DANIEL
~ THE BELOVED ~

BY THE

REV. WILLIAM M. TAYLOR, D.D.

AMBASSADOR

BELFAST ◆ GREENVILLE
NORTHERN IRELAND   SOUTH CAROLINA

Daniel The Beloved

First Published 1878
This edition 1997

ISBN   1 898787 26 3

AMBASSADOR PRODUCTIONS LTD,
Providence House
16 Hillview Avenue,
Belfast, BT5 6JR
Northern Ireland

Emerald House,
1 Chick Springs Road, Suite 206
Greenville,
South Carolina 29609
United States of America

Preface

The story of Daniel has long been a favourite with children; but, while giving due prominence to those chapters in his history which are particularly attractive to the young, I have sought specially to emphasise the lessons which it teaches to all who are engaged in business or in public life.

It was no part of my intention, at first, to attempt any exposition of the prophetic portions of the Book of Daniel; but, as I advanced, I found them so intimately connected with his character and position that it would have been impossible to form a correct estimate, either of the man or of his influence, without taking them into account. I have therefore given some attention to the visions which were either interpreted by Daniel or given to him; but I have no ambition to set up for an apocalyptic oracle, and have concerned myself mainly with extracting and illustrating those principles of permanent importance which seem to me to underlie the prophecies themselves.

For the rest, I lay this book where I have laid the others, at my Master's feet, and pray that He may use it for the fostering and encouragement of Biblical exposition in the pulpits, and of Biblical study in the closets, of the land.

New York
5 West Thirty-fifth Street.

Contents

DANIEL THE BELOVED.

I.

DANIEL AT COLLEGE.

DANIEL i., 1-21.

IN entering upon a short series of discourses on the life
of Daniel, I must take for granted the genuineness and
authenticity of the book which has been called by his name.
I am aware, indeed, that the predictions contained in this
portion of Scripture are so minute, and have been so exact-
ly fulfilled, that many have not hesitated to affirm that they
must have been written after the occurrence of the events to
which they refer. But the raising of objections by adversaries has only had the effect of establishing beyond the possibility of doubt the claims which have been put forth on
behalf of this book by all earnest believers in its credibility.
Those who wish to see what rationalistic writers have had
to say against it, from the days of Porphyry, in the third
century, down to those of the Essayists and Reviewers of
the present generation, and how their arguments have been
successfully repelled, even on the ground of criticism, may
consult Dr. Pusey's "Lectures on Daniel the Prophet,"*

* "Daniel the Prophet. Nine Lectures, delivered in the Divinity
School of the University of Oxford," by the Rev. E. B. Pusey, D.D.

while such as have not access to that masterly work, by one of the most accomplished Hebrew scholars in the world, may find an excellent summary of both sides of the argument in the introduction to Mr. Barnes's commentary on Daniel.*

But, satisfactory as all such treatises are, the humble Christian needs no stronger assurance of the genuineness of this portion of the Old Testament canon than that which is afforded by the fact that our Lord himself refers to Daniel by name, and makes special allusion to his predictions in his own prophecy concerning the destruction of Jerusalem.† This is enough. We believe in him who was and is himself "*the truth*," and with us his word is a termination of all strife.

Without further preliminary, therefore, we proceed to our labor, anticipating from it both the purest pleasure and the richest profit.

In the days of Josiah, King of Judah, the sovereignty of Western Asia was a matter of fierce contention between the monarchies of Egypt and Babylon, and the southern portion of Palestine, as lying between the two opponents, was placed in a position of peculiar difficulty. The Jewish king‡ refused to allow Pharaoh Necho a passage through his dominions, and went out to Megiddo, on the plain of Esdraelon, to oppose his progress, with his army. Here his forces were routed, and he himself was slain. He was succeeded by his younger son Jehoahaz, but, probably because he shared his father's antipathy to the Egyptians, Necho deposed him at the end of three months, and placed his elder brother Eliakim on the throne, changing his name into Jehoiakim.

---

* "Notes on the Book of Daniel," by Rev. Albert Barnes.
† See Matt. xxiv., 15, 16.
‡ 2 Kings xxiii., 29, 30 ; 2 Chron. xxxiii., 20-24.

This monarch began to reign somewhere about 609 B.C. He was, of course, a vassal of the Egyptian empire, and had to lay upon his people heavy taxes for the payment of tribute to the conquerors, in addition to those which were required for the ordinary expenses of his own government.* In the third year of his reign, however, Nabopolassar, the Assyrian emperor, gave a portion of his army to his son Nebuchadnezzar, who marched against the Egyptians, defeated them at Carchemish, and drove Pharaoh Necho out of Asia.† Thence the conqueror proceeded directly to Jerusalem, which he took after a short siege.

At first, he seems to have intended to deal very summarily with Jehoiakim, for he bound him with fetters to send him away to Babylon,‡ but eventually he changed his mind, and restored the crown to him as a vassal of his empire. Still, he took the most valuable of the vessels that were in the temple of Jehovah, and carried with him to his eastern capital several young men, belonging most probably to the principal families of Jerusalem, that they might be hostages for the good behavior of the rest of their countrymen.§

Three years after this, however, Jehoiakim rebelled against Nebuchadnezzar, who, occupied with more important affairs, left the subjugation of Palestine to the neighboring tribes. These ravished the whole country, and shut up Jehoiakim in Jerusalem;‖ and during this siege Jehoiakim was slain, and his unhonored remains were "buried with the burial of an ass," according to the word of the prophet Jeremiah.¶

He was succeeded by Jechonias, called also Jehoiachin, who reigned only three months, for, at the end of that time, Nebuchadnezzar carried him and all the royal family, the re-

---

* 2 Kings xxiii., 31–35; 2 Chron. xxxvi., 1-6.
† Jer. xlvi., 2.   ‡ 2 Chron. xxxvi., 6.   § Dan. i., 3.
‖ 2 Kings xxiv., 2.   ¶ Jer. xxii., 18, 19; xxxvi., 30, 31.

maining treasures, the strength of the army, and the princes,
and all the more useful artisans, to Babylon.* Over the
remnant of the kingdom, the Assyrian monarch made Zedekiah, one of the sons of Josiah, king; but in his stubborn self-
will, and against the advice of Jeremiah, that prince attempted, in the ninth year of his reign, to assert his independence,
with the result that Jerusalem was again besieged and taken.
The king was seized, his children were slain in his sight, his
eyes were put out, and he was led away, blind and bereaved,
into a foreign land.† Nay, more; Nebuzar-adan, the com-
mander-in-chief of the conquering army, utterly destroyed the
holy city: "they burnt the house of God, and brake down
the wall of Jerusalem, and burnt all the palaces thereof with
fire, and destroyed all the goodly vessels thereof. And them
that escaped the sword carried he away to Babylon; where
they were servants to him and his sons until the reign of the
kingdom of Persia."‡ There were thus, if I may so express
it, three distinct instalments of captives carried away to the
land of Babylon: first, the young men taken in the third
year of the reign of Jehoiakim; second, the large number
removed along with Jehoiachin; and, third, those who accompanied Zedekiah after the Jewish capital had been laid
waste.

Daniel was one of those who were first removed; and
with him were three others, whose names are specially recorded, because they were like-minded with him, and because they afterward played no mean part in maintaining
their integrity at the risk of all that men commonly hold
dear. Daniel appears to have been of noble birth, for he
is spoken of as belonging to the royal family;§ and at the

---

* 2 Kings xxiv., 10–16. See, also, articles JEHOIAKIM and JEHOIA-
CHIN, Smith's "Bible Dictionary."

† 2 Kings xxv., 1–7.

‡ 2 Chron. xxxvi., 19, 20; 2 Kings xxv., 8–10.   § Dan. i., 3.

time of his removal to Babylon, he must have been of a very tender age. The last verse of the first chapter of his book informs us that he continued even unto the first year of King Cyrus; and his latest vision* is dated in the third year of Cyrus. Thus he lived in Babylonia at least three years longer than the seventy years of the Captivity, counting these, as many believe they should be reckoned, from the third year of Jehoiakim. Supposing, therefore, that at the time of his last vision he had reached the venerable age of eighty-seven, this would make him a boy of fourteen when he was taken from Jerusalem. This conjecture is somewhat confirmed by incidental glimpses which we get in classic authors into the customs of Eastern monarchs. Thus Plato,† speaking of the Persians, says, "After twice seven years have passed, those whom they call royal instructors receive the boys to educate." Add three years, during which we know that Daniel and his friends were under training, and this would bring him to the age of seventeen. But, according to Xenophon, sixteen or seventeen was the age of the adults at which they entered upon the king's service. If, therefore, this supposition be accepted, we may conceive what an affliction his departure from Jerusalem would be to his parents' hearts, and with what earnest, prayerful solicitude (for his must have been a godly home) they would follow him in thought to Babylon, and shield him with their supplications from the dangers and temptations to which he would be exposed. And, as we shall see, their holy training and loving petitions were not fruitless.

He and his three friends before alluded to were, with others, chosen by Ashpenaz, the chief of the eunuchs, to be trained in a special royal seminary for the service of the king. They received Babylonian names, and were to be

---

* Dan. x., 1.   † Pusey's "Lectures," pp. 16, 17.

instructed in all the learning of the Chaldeans, so as to be
fitted for posts of usefulness in the empire.   Dr. Kitto has
described a similar method of procedure with young slaves,
as having been customary at the Turkish court up to a com-
paratively recent date.   I must quote his words :

"The time is still within living memory when the pages
of the seraglio, the officers of the court, as well as the greater part of the high functionaries of state and governors of
provinces, were originally boys of Christian parentage, who
had been taken captive in war, or bought, or stolen in time
of peace.   The finest and most capable of these were sent
to the palace, and placed under the charge of the chief of
the white eunuchs.   These lads were brought up in the religion of their masters, and in a school within the palace
they received such complete instruction in Turkish learning
and science as it was the lot of few others to obtain.   Much
pains were taken to teach them to speak the Turkish language with the greatest purity, as spoken at court.   They
were clad neatly and well, but temperately dieted.   They
slept in large dormitories, where there were long rows of
beds.   When they reached a proper age, they were instructed in military discipline, and it was an aim to render them
active, brave, and laborious.   Every one was also, according
to the custom of the country, taught some handicraft employment, to serve him as a resource in any time of need.
Their education being completed, those who had shown
most capacity were employed about the person of the sovereign, and the rest were assigned to the various offices of
the extensive establishment to which they belonged.   In
due time these able or successful youths got advanced to
high court offices, which gave them immediate access to the
royal person, an advantage which soon paved the way to
their going out on military commands, or to take the government of provinces.   It has not rarely happened that fa-

vored court officers have at once stepped into the highest
offices of the State, without having been previously abroad
in the world as pachas or military commanders."*

Daniel and his companions were, in a word, the young
cadets of their times, differing from their modern representatives mainly in this, that they were captives deprived, in
some respects, of their liberty, and held for the service of an
alien emperor in a foreign land.

The arrangements of the seminary or college, however,
were of such a nature as involved the Hebrew youths in immediate difficulty. The food for the pupils was supplied
from the royal table; and as, according to the Jewish law,
only certain animals were accounted clean, and even these
had to be slain in such a manner as to leave no blood in
the flesh before they could be eaten, it must be at once apparent that, if they partook, along with their classmates, of
the things which were provided, they would be guilty of vio-
lating the precepts of the Mosaic code. Besides, it was a
custom among the heathen to bring a portion of that which
was eaten and drunk by them as an oblation to the gods,
and sometimes also they used for food animals that had
already been offered at the altar of their gods.

It is possible, therefore, that Daniel and his friends may
have felt that in partaking of such articles of diet they
would be giving countenance to idolatry; or perhaps, as
Calvin suggests, they may have resolved to abstain on the
principle of prudence, believing that the opportunity of self-
indulgence was a temptation, and desiring to keep themselves as far as possible from danger. To me, however, it
rather seems, from the fact that the term "defile" is used,
that their scruple was a religious one, and was in some way

---

* Kitto's "Daily Bible Readings," Evening Series, Twenty-third
Week, Seventh Day.

connected with their nationality. In any case, the purpose
was steadfastly made by Daniel that he would not partake
of anything that came from the king's table, and his three
friends concurred with him in his resolution. It was a matter of conscience with them, and they were determined to
abide by their convictions at whatever cost.

This purpose is the more to be admired when we take
into account their youth, their condition as captives, and the
effect which their disobedience of the king's orders might
have produced. If we have been correct in supposing that
the lads were all as yet in their teens, then it was very much
to their credit, and spoke much for the character of their
early home-training, that they had any deep religious convictions at all, much more that they were resolved to stand
by them.

They might have been laughed at by their senior fellow-
students ; they might have been put down as silly boys by
those who were in authority over them ; yet, boys as they
were, they would not barter the approval of their own consciences for any considerations of comfort or security. Then
they were captives. If, therefore, the refusal to carry out
the royal injunctions would have endangered the life of the
chief of the eunuchs, much more would it put their lives in
jeopardy. Yet they were firm. They did not suppose that
the responsibility of deciding such a question was removed
from them to their master ; neither did they seek to shelter themselves under the plea that, in their circumstances,
it was necessary for them to yield. They felt that nothing
could make it necessary for them to sin. They knew that,
in the last resort, the thing came to be a matter of their own
choice, and they deliberately said that they would not defile
themselves. What did it signify, though they should ruin
their prospects in the college ? They were not to be drawn
away from their position by the enticements of self-interest,

any more than they were to be driven from it by the fear of those things with which they might be threatened for their disobedience. They were convinced that it would be wrong for them to take the food provided for them; and they would not do wrong on any pretext, or for any consideration. It was bravely resolved, and the firmness of character which they manifested is worthy of the imitation of all young men similarly circumstanced.

But, though they were quite determined, they did not attempt to carry out their purpose in a foolish and quixotic way. With a sagacity which is the prophecy of his later wisdom, Daniel went at once to the head of the department, and calmly and politely explained the case to him.

This official—partly, we may suppose, from the frank ingenuousness of Daniel himself, but principally, we are sure, from the operation of God's Spirit on his heart—had taken a great interest in the young Jew; so he listened with attention and sympathy to his request. It was not in his power, however, to give his direct sanction to the proposal which Daniel made. Had he done that, he would have forfeited his life. But, in all probability, he gave the young student to understand that if he could prevail upon Melzar, his subordinate, who was immediately over him and his companions, to comply with his wishes, he would himself wink at the irregularity, and no harm would come of it. At the same time, he may have privately counselled Melzar to look with favor on Daniel's request, and stretch a point in his behalf.

To him, accordingly, Daniel went, and proposed that the matter might be submitted to experiment. He asked that for ten days they might be permitted to live on pulse (a kind of coarse grain, or pease) and water, and if at the end of that time they seemed to have deteriorated, then he might do with them as he pleased; but if they appeared as well-favored as before, then they might be allowed to continue their abstemious diet. Melzar agreed to his proposal. The experiment was made, and it was signally successful; so they were allowed to carry out their determination with a good conscience, and they gave themselves with such ardor to their studies that, with the blessing of God upon their efforts, they made more progress than their companions; for at the end of three years, when the graduation examination was held, there were none found like them; nay, they were discovered to be ten times better in all matters of wisdom and understanding than all the magicians and all the astrologers that were in all the realm.

Many wholesome lessons may be learned from this narrative. I select only a few of the more prominent.

In the first place, we see how national sins are followed ever by divine retribution. In their victorious progress westward, the rulers of Assyria and Babylon, when they conquered any important city or territory, adopted the plan of carrying its inhabitants to one of their Eastern possessions, and of supplying the places of those who were thus removed by colonists sent from some far-distant province.* In this way they secured many important political advantages. They filled the newly annexed district with settlers on whose loyalty they could depend, thus freeing themselves from the necessity of constantly occupying it with an armed force; they peopled the great cities which they were building in the East; and, by removing the captives from their native homes, they broke up the sentiment of nationality among them; so that within two or three generations they came to be merged in the general population of the empire.

But while the Babylonians were proceeding on these plans, and acting from these motives in the case of the Jews, they were at the same time, all unconsciously to themselves,

---

* 2 Kings xvi., 6–24.

the instruments whom God was employing for the chastisement of his people, and the fulfilment of his prophecies regarding them. Listen to these words, taken from the sacred
chronicler. They describe Zedekiah's administration, but,
unhappily, they are also applicable to the doings of the people under not a few of his predecessors. "He stiffened his
neck, and hardened his heart from turning unto the Lord
God of Israel. Moreover, all the chief of the priests, and
the people, transgressed very much after all the abomina-
tions of the heathen ; and polluted the house of the Lord
which he had hallowed in Jerusalem. And the Lord God
of their fathers sent to them by his messengers, rising up be-
times, and sending ; because he had compassion on his people, and on his dwelling-place. But they mocked the messengers of God, and despised his words, and misused his
prophets, until the wrath of the Lord arose against his people, till there was no remedy. Therefore he brought upon
them the king of the Chaldees."*

Then let these sayings be compared with the words of
Moses, uttered eight hundred and sixty years before : "But
it shall come to pass, if thou wilt not hearken unto the voice
of the Lord thy God.....The Lord shall bring thee, and
thy king which thou shalt set over thee, unto a nation which
neither thou nor thy fathers have known ; and there shalt
thou serve other gods, wood and stone."†

Here, therefore, is national sin punished by national calamity, and that without any miraculous intervention of divine power, but simply in the ordinary course of Providence,
and through the operation of the free-will of men. There
is nothing exceptional in the case but the fact that it is so
fully described in this book, and that we are permitted, as
it were, to read a fragment taken from the secret volume of

---

* 2 Chron. xxxvi., 13-17.　　　† Deut. xxviii., 15, 36.

the plan of God. The same processes are going on now. We see among the nations of the earth some groaning under the consequences of iniquities which were committed by their representatives centuries ago ; and we behold others pursuing such a course of blind folly and unscrupulous selfishness as must result, sooner or later, in uttermost disaster.

It is said that nations have no conscience. In one sense that is true ; but in another, that is just the evil which I would most earnestly deprecate. There is not for the aggregate community any abstract faculty like that which sits supremely in each human breast ; but still, it is the duty of all who compose a nation to take order that they who represent them shall, in all their dealings, alike with their fellow-citizens and with other nations, act with justice, truth, honor, and wisdom ; for if they do not, they may rest assured that the day of vengeance will come, sooner or later, when God will visit either them or their descendants for their iniquities. The truest patriot, therefore, is ever the most rigid in his demands that " the rulers shall be just, ruling in the fear of the Lord ;" and when people and magistrates together unite " to mock the messengers of God and to despise his words," you may write Ichabod on that nation's banner, and put *Finis* to its history, for its glory will be departed, and its existence ended.

In the second place, we see here most admirably illustrated the duty of adhering in all circumstances to that course of conduct which in our consciences we believe to be right. It is always right to do right. That may seem to be a truism, yet it is very far from being universally acted upon. Men will frequently admit that a thing in the abstract is duty, and then persuade themselves to do the opposite, with the plea that in their circumstances they could not help themselves. But no circumstances can make that right which is in its own nature wrong. It never can be

necessary to sin.   No doubt we may say that if we refuse
to sin under certain pressure, death will be the result.   But
that will not alter the case; for it is better to die than to
sin ; and if there be no other way out of it, we ought to be
willing to die rather than to sin.

Is not this the lesson of the entire martyrology of the
Church?   And are we worthy of the privileges which others
purchased for us with their blood if we refuse to follow their
example?   If ever young men could say that circumstances
warranted them in yielding up their convictions, Daniel and
his companions were these young men; yet they did not
make any such excuse, and so the very difficulty of their
position only brought their nobleness more conspicuously
to view.

But in putting the case that death would be the consequence of refusing to sin, I have somewhat overstated it.
Frequently, indeed, death has been the result ; but it is not
always so.   It was not so in the instance before us.   God
opened the way before these youths, and made it easier for
them to follow the dictates of their consciences than perhaps, at first, they feared it would be.   And it is often thus.
Indeed, we may say that the difficulties in the way of the
discharge of duty are rarely so formidable in the actual
encounter as they seemed to be in the anticipation.   When
God says, "Go forward," then, as we advance, that which appeared to be—nay, which really was—a sea of trouble is divided before us, and he leads us through on dry land.   The
slothful man says, "There is a lion in the path ;" but the in-
dustrious man advances to discover that it is only a harmless
shrub, which, in the gray twilight of the morning, his neigh-
bor's fears have magnified into the likeness of the king of
the forest.   In like manner, the weak-willed one who yields
to temptation, saying, "I could not do otherwise," exagger-
ates the difficulties of resisting ; while the brave-souled be-

liever, as he presses on, discovers that the obstacles recede before him, and he has a clear path all through.

Let us be admonished, therefore, by the example of these youths. Especially let the young people before me take heart from the record of the manner in which God prepared the way for Daniel. Away from home, at school, or college, or business, you may miss the friendly counsel of Christian companions, and the wise directions and loving fellowship of parents, and may feel it hard to be left entirely on your own resources, with no one to consult in times of perplexity. Yet you have God to go to, and he will be for you if you will be for him. Stand, then, on your convictions, and make your appeal to him for help. Have you never read these words, "When a man's ways please the Lord, he maketh even his enemies to be at peace with him?" They mean something. There is scarcely one Christian here who has come to middle life but can tell you some chapter of his own history that will corroborate their truth. Courage, then, my young brothers! Do only and always that which is right, and you will often find that where you had feared there was a yawning chasm and a foaming torrent to cross, God had already provided for you a bridge.

In the third place, we have in this history an illustration of the value of temperance in eating and drinking. It is supposed by many that a luxurious diet is necessary to health, and not seldom men use intoxicating drink as a constant beverage, under the delusion that it imparts strength. But both of these mistakes are exposed in the narrative before us. A sparing diet is conducive to health and long life, while the pampering of the appetite with many dainties tends to the production of disease. Then, as regards strong drink, we have the testimony of medical men of highest standing to the fact that it is not necessary to a healthy person, and that its habitual use is always more or less injurious. Hence, if for no other reason, we might well abstain from it as an article of diet. But when we take into account the insidious nature of alcohol, which always creates a craving for itself, and, above all, when we think of the numbers in the land who are continually falling under its power, and of the fearful amount of misery and crime which is traceable directly or indirectly to its influence, we may surely be brought to adopt the course of Daniel and his friends in regard to it, the rather as no evil consequences will follow the carrying-out of such a resolution.

Do not say to me that there is no danger of you. It is he who thinketh he standeth here who has most need to take heed lest he fall. You may find among the helpless, almost hopeless, drunkards on our streets many who once said the same thing as you are now saying, and who seemed then to have as good ground for saying it as you have now. Why, then, should you imagine that you are in this respect infallible?

You may reply again, as some have done, that if there were any certainty that you would become a drunkard you would abstain. But to that I answer, in the words of Butler, "Probability is the guide of life." You guard against probabilities, nay, even against mere possibilities, in other things; why not also in this? You have no certainty that your house shall take fire, yet, as a prudent man, you insure it, and your furniture too; you have no positive knowledge that your ship shall be lost at sea, yet, as a wise man, you underwrite it to the full. So abstinence from strong drink is an insurance against intemperance, with this advantage—that the premium goes not into the coffers of a wealthy company, but comes back to yourself in the shape of pecuniary saving, physical health, and domestic comfort.

But I care not to put this question on such selfish ground. I ask you to look at it in the light of the multitudes whom

strong drink is beguiling to their ruin. Will you not abstain,
if thereby you may remove temptation out of their way, and
help them to restoration? There is no hope for them save
in abstaining. But should not we assist them by the moral
influence of our fellowship with them in so doing? When
David thirsted for the water of the well of Bethlehem, and
his three mighty men broke through the enemy's ranks and
returned with a pitcherful of it, he would not drink it. Men's
lives had been jeoparded for it! So he poured it out before the Lord. In like manner, when the wine-cup is presented to you, think of the multitudes of souls which are not
merely imperilled, but destroyed, by that bewitching draught,
and then you, too, will pour it out before the Lord, saying,
"It is good neither to eat flesh, nor to drink wine, nor to do
anything whereby a brother stumbleth, or is offended, or is
made weak."

Finally, we may see here how God's hand is in all his
people's concerns. He gave Daniel favor in the eyes of
Ashpenaz, and he gave him and his three friends "knowledge and skill in all learning and wisdom." Doubtless all
this had been made matter of prayer by the youths themselves; yet it is interesting to note how it is here so simply
and sublimely recognized. And are not we taught by this
to consult God about everything? Let those who are far
from home ask God to bring them to the knowledge of
some safe and sagacious friends. Let those who are in per-
plexing care ask God to give them light. Let the man of
business make request to God for guidance in the difficulties that daily meet him. Let the housewife go to him with
her domestic trials. Let the very school-boys among us ask
God to assist them in their evening studies. Did you ever
think of that, my children? Your sums would be done by
you more diligently; your hard sentences would be con-
strued by you with more interest; your very satchels would

sit more lightly on your shoulders, and your steps as you go forth to school would be more joyous, if you would only reverently and confidingly ask God to help you in your education. Try it, from this time forward ; and so the story of Daniel's college life will be to you a perennial blessing.

II.

THE FORGOTTEN DREAM.

DANIEL ii., 1–23.

THE events recorded in the second chapter of the Book
of Daniel are there said to have occurred in the second year of the reign of Nebuchadnezzar. Now, as in the
first verse of the same book it is affirmed that Daniel and
his friends were taken captives from Jerusalem in the third
year of Jehoiakim, and as, in the twenty-fifth chapter of Jeremiah, the fourth of Jehoiakim is identified with the first of
Nebuchadnezzar, a chronological difficulty is created, which,
as usual, has been made the most of by the antagonists of
the Sacred Scriptures. If, say they, Daniel was taken to
Babylon in the third of Jehoiakim, and was subsequently
three years in training at the royal college, how could the
events narrated in this chapter have occurred in the second year of Nebuchadnezzar, if at least Jeremiah is right in
speaking of the fourth of Jehoiakim as the first of Nebuchadnezzar?

Different solutions of this question have been proposed,
the most probable being that adopted by Milman, Pusey,
Stuart, and other similar expositors, who suppose that Nebuchadnezzar reigned for some time conjointly with his father, Nabopolassar, and that Jeremiah reckons the commencement of his reign from the beginning of that association, while Daniel counts it from the time when, after Nabopolassar's death, Nebuchadnezzar became sole monarch.
Some foundation for this view is furnished by Berosus, the

historian, who states that Nabopolassar, being infirm, gave
up his army to his son, who, having defeated the Egyptians
at Carchemish, marched on to Jerusalem and took it. But
whether this explanation be accounted satisfactory or not,
the very existence of such a difficulty becomes, when rightly
looked at, a proof of the good faith of the writer. A forger
would not deliberately introduce difficulties, but would take
particular care to avoid anything like discrepancies between
his statements and those made in books already existing
and received as authoritative. Now we know, from the
ninth chapter of Daniel, that the author of this book represents Daniel as a diligent student of the prophecies of Jeremiah, and it is utterly inconceivable in such circumstances
that an impostor would introduce here a date that seems to
be at variance with one given by Jeremiah. Hence we must
conclude, that what appears to be a discrepancy to us
would present no difficulty to those who lived at the time,
and is susceptible of some such explanation as that which I
have given.

But, leaving this question of dates, let us proceed to the
narrative itself. Nebuchadnezzar, by his victory over Pharaoh and his capture of Jerusalem, had enlarged his dominions up to the Mediterranean Sea, and it is natural to suppose that he must have thought much and long upon the probable future of the empire which he had thus extended. No
one can be altogether insensible to the after-destiny of anything in the acquisition or construction of which he has been
specially interested. Men may deny the existence of a future state, but they never think of doubting that history will
go on developing itself after they have left the world, even
as it did before they appeared on the earth, and while they
lived upon it. Hence, whatever their religious opinions may
be, they cannot shut out of their minds all consideration of
the future fate of that with which through life they have been

greatly concerned, but which they must, sooner or later, leave behind them.

We are all more or less conscious of this in our own little concerns; and we try, by some testamentary deed, to provide as far as possible that the things in which we delighted shall pass into the hands of those who shall think well both of us and them. The man of science cannot contemplate with any satisfaction the idea of the various specimens in his museum being scattered among strangers, so he contrives to leave his collection, as a whole, to some public institution, linking his name with his legacy, that he may keep himself from being forgotten. The scholar or theologian does the same with his library, and the man of taste acts on a similar principle with his gallery of pictures. Much in the same way the ambitious conqueror, whose heart is set upon the empire which he has made, desires to forecast its future. He wishes, perhaps, to found a dynasty, or he seeks, in some way, to secure the perpetuity of his kingdom as a whole, in order that he may be spoken of always as its founder.

Now, active, scheming, vigorous, and unscrupulous as Nebuchadnezzar was, we may be sure that these subjects were often pondered by him; and on one occasion, when, as he lay upon his bed, he had been thinking specially "what should come to pass hereafter," he fell asleep and dreamed a curious dream, which somehow peculiarly impressed him as having an intimate connection with the train of thought which he had been prosecuting. Indeed, he regarded it as being in some sort an indication from Heaven of the future, concerning which he was so anxious.

Nor was this idea altogether unnatural, for, among all nations, at that time, it was generally supposed that dreams were one of the media through which divine revelations were made, and there were everywhere recognized men of learning, whose special office it was to interpret such visions.

Homer, in a well-known passage in his "Iliad,"* says that a dream is from Jupiter, and elsewhere he relates how the mind of Jove was communicated to Agamemnon in a vision. I do not imagine, indeed, that the ancient heathens would account every dream as worthy of attention ; but when, as in the present instance, the vision came to the most important and exalted person in the nation, and made such an impression upon him, that he was troubled and overawed in spirit, they would at once conclude that there was some special significance in it, and that it was to be viewed as a divine revelation. We cannot affirm that they were always right in regarding particular dreams as from the Lord, but that they were sometimes correct is evident from the cases of Pharaoh and Nebuchadnezzar ; and even yet it is a question very difficult to answer in a definite manner, whether any significance, or, if any, how much, is to be attributed to the visions of the night.

We all allow that God may, and does, influence the workings of our minds through the operation of the laws of suggestion or association while we are awake ; for it is impossible to hold in any intelligible fashion the doctrine of the agency of the Holy Spirit unless we make such an admission. But if God can thus influence our minds when we are awake, it is equally easy for him to do so while we sleep, so that there is no antecedent impossibility against the view that there may be something in dreams, after all.

Again, the providence of God must take cognizance of our dreams equally with our waking thoughts, and must be equally over both, if, at least, we are to conceive of it as really universal. Hence there is nothing absurd or unphilosophical in supposing that God may avail himself of the phenomena of dreams for the purpose of turning the mind to

---

* "Iliad," i., 63.

his truth or leading it in some particular direction. How far he does this, it is impossible to say. But I have read and heard so many well-authenticated anecdotes which told of singular things—call them coincidences or what you will —in reference to dreams, that I would hesitate to affirm that there is never anything whatever in them ; while, on the other hand, so much nonsense, superstition, trickery, and deceit have been connected with dreams and their fancied interpretation, that one hesitates equally to admit that there is anything in them. In the autobiography of Lord Brougham there is told a marvellous story of an experience of this kind which that noble lord had in early life, and which is vouched for by himself. One of his early companions had made an agreement with him, in reckless joke, that in order to set at rest the question of a future state, the first of them to die should, if there was reality in the after-life, appear to the survivor, and enlighten him on the subject. Years passed away ; his friend went to India, and one evening as Brougham was in his bath he fell into a brief sleep and dreamed that he saw his former companion, who assured him that there was a future state, for he had now entered upon it. Months afterward he received intelligence of his friend's death, and on making investigation discovered that it must have occurred about the very time of his own dream. On this Brougham remarks : " Singular coincidence ! Yet, when one reflects on the vast number of dreams which, night after night, pass through our brains, the number of coincidences between the vision and the event are, perhaps, fewer and less remarkable than a fair calculation of chances would warrant us to expect. Nor is it surprising, considering the variety of our thoughts in sleep, and that they all bear some analogy to the affairs of life, that a dream should sometimes coincide with a contemporaneous, or even with a future, event. This is not much more wonderful than that a person whom we had no reason to expect should appear to us at the very moment we had been thinking or speaking of him; yet so common is this that it has for ages grown into a proverb."*

Some may be disposed to go even farther than his lordship, but, for my part, I prefer to leave the whole thing unsolved. Sleep is a mystery, and dreams are a mystery. What wonder, therefore, that many problems concerning both should baffle our ingenuity to explain? We apply to this subject the words of Hamlet in reference to apparitions: "There are more things in heaven and earth than are dreamt of in our philosophy;" and whatever may be the case with dreams in general, we have at least the highest authority for believing that, in the present instance, Nebuchadnezzar was right in regarding his vision as from the Lord.

But though he had a profound impression of the importance of his dream, he was quite unable to recall it when he awoke. This is not so peculiar an experience as to need any special remark. We have all had similar things happen to ourselves in regard, not only to the visions of the night, but to waking realities. Every one knows what it is to have forgotten a name, which, in spite of all his efforts to recall it, will not come at his command, but which he recognizes in a moment when it is suggested to him by another. And many a musician can tell that frequently he has been unable to raise a tune which he had formerly known, but which he recognized at once when it was struck up by another. But, as still more closely analogous to the case of Nebuchadnezzar here, I quote two instances. The first I have met with in the course of my reading in mental philosophy, but I have been unable, after long search through my

---

* "Autobiography of Henry, Lord Brougham," vol. i., pp. 146–148. Harper & Brothers, New York.

library, to lay my hands upon the authority ;* the second I take from the biography of the poet Coleridge. A gentleman connected with the bar had a very difficult case in hand, and as the day for the trial drew near his mind was continuously dwelling upon it. One morning during this period, he happened to say to his wife at the breakfast-table that he had, in his dreams, delivered a clear opinion on the cause, and that he would give a great deal if he could recall the argument which had then passed through his mind, as he believed it to be thoroughly convincing. His wife smiled, and said that if he went to his writing-table, and opened a particular drawer, she fancied he would find it fully written out. Then she explained that, in his sleep, he had risen and gone to his desk, and sat down to write ; and that she, fearing something had gone wrong with him, had followed, but, finding that he was engaged at his desk, had watched in silence until he had finished. He hastened to his study, and, in glancing over the paper, recognized in a moment the argument to which he had referred.

The incident in Coleridge's life refers to the composition of his metrical fragment, entitled " Kubla Khan," which, he says, came to him during sleep, into which he fell while reading in " Purchas's Pilgrims." He continued for about three hours apparently in sleep, during which he had the most vivid impression that he had composed between two and three hundred lines. "The images," he says, "rose up before me as things with a parallel production of the correspondent expressions, without any sensation or consciousness of effort." On awaking, he had so distinct a remembrance of the whole, that he seized his pen and wrote down the fragment which is still preserved. Unfortunately,

---

* Since the above was written, I have discovered it, viz., Abercrombie's "Intellectual Powers," p. 222.

however, he was called away to attend to some business. The interruption lasted more than an hour, and, on his return to his study, he found, to his intense surprise and mortification, that, though he still retained some vague and dim recollection of the general purport of the vision, yet, with the exception of some eight or ten scattered lines and images, all the rest had passed away, like the images on the surface of a stream into which a stone had been cast. Thus the thing had gone from him, as in the case before us.*

But Nebuchadnezzar thought that he had a sure resource to fall back upon. There were in his realm magicians, astrologers, sorcerers, and Chaldeans, who professed to be able, from the practice of various arts, to furnish the interpretation of any dream ; and the king, believing that if they could correctly explain a vision, they could also accurately reproduce that which he had seen, sent for them, and told the circumstances in which he was placed, at the same time informing them that if they failed in making known to him both the dream and its interpretation, they should be put to death in the most shameful manner, and their houses razed to the foundation ; while, if they succeeded, they should be loaded with honors and rewards.

This procedure on the part of the monarch has been much blamed ; and, indeed, so far as regards the harshness and severity of the sentence which he pronounced in case of the failure of the wise men, there is nothing to be said in its defence. We must only bear in mind that he was an Oriental despot, and that the cruelty of this decree is quite in keeping with his treatment of Daniel's three friends afterward, and with his brutality to Zedekiah, the King of Judah. Unhappily, such capricious and utterly inhuman out-

---

* See Coleridge's "Complete Works," edited by Professor Shedd, vol. vii., p. 212.

rages were by no means uncommon in the East, and are
even yet far too largely practised by the Persian, Indian,
and Turkish rulers.

So far, however, as his demand that the wise men should
reproduce the dream is concerned, we cannot see that Nebuchadnezzar was at fault; for if they, by divine assistance,
or even by human skill, could tell infallibly what a dream
meant, it was quite as easy for them to tell the dream itself.
But had they made the attempt, they knew that they would
certainly have been detected as impostors.   Hence they exclaimed against his demand.   They alleged that he was asking a new and preposterous thing, and affirmed that there
was none that could show what he wanted, save the gods,
whose dwelling was not with flesh.

This, however, only exasperated the king the more, and
made him at once issue the decree which he had threatened.   Nay, such was his fury that he required the captain
of his guard to proceed at once to the wholesale massacre
of the wise men; and, as it would seem, the butchery had
been actually carried on for some time before Daniel became aware of the events out of which it arose; for it was
only when Arioch came to lead him and his companions
out to execution that he discovered what had occurred.
He complained of the unseemly haste of the king, and of
the grievous injustice of putting him and his friends to
death before they had had an opportunity of trying to comply with the royal request as to the interpretation of his
dream.   He further desired that time should be given, and
promised that he would furnish what Nebuchadnezzar
wanted.

Had the matter been one in which the king was less interested, it is questionable if any effect would have been
produced by this expostulation.   Very likely Arioch would
have said, "It is too late now.   I have to obey orders, or

lose my own life." But, knowing that, above and beyond all other things, Nebuchadnezzar desired to understand the meaning of his dream, Arioch hastened to inform the monarch that he had come upon one of the Jewish captives who professed to be able to interpret his vision, and whose only stipulations were that the needful time should be granted, and that the massacre of the wise men should be stayed. To these terms the monarch readily consented ; and Daniel, telling his three friends of the responsibility which he had taken upon him, engaged them to pray earnestly on his behalf, or, as it is phrased in the narrative, " to desire mercies of the God of heaven concerning this secret."

In answer to this united prayer, the vision was revealed to Daniel, as it had been to Nebuchadnezzar, in his sleep ; and the first thing he did when he awoke was to offer an appropriate thanksgiving to God, who had thus highly favored him. Then he went to Arioch, who introduced him to the king ; and, first of all, disclaiming in the most explicit terms that he had received the secret "for any wisdom that he had more than any living," and giving the entire glory to God, whose he was and whom he served, he rehearsed the vision, and gave the interpretation in such a way as to satisfy the monarch that he had reached the truth.

Keeping to his word, the king honored him with many great gifts, and made him ruler over the whole province of Babylon, and chief of the governors over all the wise men. But Daniel would have no " lonely glory." His three friends, by their prayers, had helped him to his exaltation, and, at his request, they also were set over the affairs of the empire, though he himself held the foremost place at the court, or gate of the king, and was, in modern phrase, Grand Vizier of the Porte of Babylon.

I have not given either a description of the vision itself, or of its explanation by the prophet, my main business in

these discourses being with the incidents of Daniel's life
and their lessons; but it may be interesting and instructive
to take a rapid survey of them both, and this I shall attempt
to do in my next lecture. Meanwhile we cannot fail to be
reminded by all this history of another captive, who, for his
interpretation of royal dreams, was raised to the second position in the Egyptian realm; and it is interesting to note
the marks of resemblance and difference between the two.

Joseph and Daniel were alike in that they were both men
of incorruptible fidelity and devout humility; and they stand
out in Jewish history—the one at its beginning, and the
other near its close—as men in whom few, if any, defects
of character or blemishes of conduct appear. As Auberlen
has beautifully said, "They were both representatives of
the true God and his people at heathen courts; both were
exemplary in their pure walk before the Lord; both were
endowed with the gift of bringing into clear light the dim
presentiments of truth which express themselves among the
heathen in God-sent dreams; both were gifted with marvellous wisdom and insight, and, for this reason, highly honored by the powers of this world. They represent the call-
ing of Israel to be a holy people, a royal priesthood among
the nations, and the final end of the Old Testament theocracy to lead to one universal is clearly shown forth by their
history. Thus, also, they are types of Christ, the true Israel, and types of the destiny of their nation by which it
would be a light to lighten the Gentiles..... Daniel, in
every respect more visibly blessed than Joseph, is the most
prominent figure and the greatest character in the last centuries of the Old Covenant, the most excellent example of a
true Israelite. Such a man was called to be the apocalyptic
prophet of the Old Testament. And since we know that
the prophet of the New Testament was the disciple whom
Jesus loved, the circumstance that God has chosen two of

the best men under the Old and New Covenants to receive
and record his Apocalypses must fill us with deep reverence
for their apocalyptic revelations."*

But now, turning to the practical improvement of this narrative, we have set before us, in the first place, the value of
united prayer. When Daniel undertook the solution of the
difficulty which Nebuchadnezzar had brought before the
wise men, he engaged his three friends to pray earnestly on
his behalf, and we may be sure that he was fervent in supplication on his own account. He believed in God as the
hearer of prayer. Wise as he was, he was not too wise to
make request to God; nay, rather he consecrated his wisdom by combining it with piety. Probably he remembered
how, in the ancient history of his people, Aaron and Hur
had stayed up the hands of Moses, and he wished to be
strengthened similarly by the prayers of his companions.
The issue showed that he had acted wisely.

We are reminded by it of an interesting episode in the
history of the Westminster Assembly of Divines. When
that learned company was engaged in the composition of
the Shorter Catechism, and had come to the question "What
is God?" no one would attempt to furnish an answer. At
length, as a way out of the difficulty, and without knowing
who the person was that might be appointed, they agreed
that the youngest man present should be required to write
the answer. When they discovered who he was, there was
still the same shrinking in his heart, but at length he agreed
to do as his brethren wished, provided they would permit
him to retire, and would promise that all the time he was
away they would pray for the divine assistance to be ac-
corded to him. They did so, and in a short while he re-

---

* "Daniel and the Revelation," by Carl August Auberlen, translated
by Rev. A. Saphir, pp. 23, 24.

turned with that answer with which we are all familiar, and the comprehensive brevity and clearness of which have awakened the admiration of every thoughtful mind.

Now, it would be well if, when we are in difficulty as to the path of duty, or in severe trial, or in prospect of arduous labor, we would secure that a band of friends should pray on our behalf. Depend upon it, "more things are wrought by prayer than the world dreams of." These words of Jesus, "If any two of you shall agree on earth as touching anything which ye shall ask in my name, it shall be given you," constitute the charter of the prayer-meeting. There is a special promise to united prayer. "The effectual fervent prayer of a righteous man availeth much;" but the united prayers of a company of like-minded believers avail more. Indeed, as the poet has said, "The whole round earth is bound by prayer about the feet of God." Let us, then, endeavor to secure that our friends are given to prayer; for if they can help us in no other way, they can help us in the best of all ways—by their united supplications on our behalf.

But, in the second place, we have an illustration here of the workings of gratitude. The moment he had received the revelation, and ere yet he went with it to Nebuchadnezzar, Daniel poured out his heart in thanksgiving to God. He "blessed the God of heaven," saying, "Blessed be the name of God for ever and ever: for wisdom and might are his: and he changeth the times and the seasons: he removeth kings, and setteth up kings: he giveth wisdom unto the wise, and knowledge to them that know understanding: he revealeth the deep and secret things: he knoweth what is in the darkness, and the light dwelleth with him. I thank thee, and praise thee, O thou God of my fathers, who hast given me wisdom and might, and hast made known unto me what we desired of thee: for thou hast now made known unto us the king's matter."

How many, when they have got the blessing for which they asked, forget to be grateful for it! "Were there not ten cleansed, but where are the nine?" We cry when we are in extremity; but when the terror passes, we forget to give thanks to him who has removed its cause. Let the conduct of Daniel here shame us for our ingratitude to God for the many blessings which in answer to our prayers he has bestowed upon us; and let us seek to show our thanks, not only in the utterance of words, but also in the offering of our hearts and lives as incense unto him.

In the third place, we have here an illustration of the devout humility of genuine piety. Daniel is careful to let Nebuchadnezzar understand that he has not received the secret from God for any excellence about himself. He fears to stand between the king and Jehovah. He gives all the glory to the Most High. There is always a modesty about true greatness, and you may know whether or not piety is genuine by inquiring if it be characterized by humility. The good man will never seek to hide God from the view of his fellow-men. He will endeavor to make his light shine, but he will not make it shine so as to draw attention to himself. He will arrange it so that its rays will all converge in God, and men shall glorify the Father in heaven.

See how beautifully John the Baptist was clothed with that humility. When the Jews came to him, asking, "Who art thou?" and almost importuning him to answer that he was the Messiah, he would not yield to their desire, but said, "I am not the Messiah, but I am sent before him to prepare his way;" and when, afterward, men sought to provoke his envy of Jesus by telling him how the prophet of Nazareth was attracting more followers than he, his only answer was, "He must increase, but I must decrease!"

So, again, when Paul was writing to the church at Corinth, he manifested the same beautiful humility, saying,

"Who then is Paul, and who is Apollos, but ministers by whom ye believed, even as the Lord gave to every man? I have planted, Apollos watered; but God gave the increase. So then neither is he that planteth anything, neither he that watereth; but God that giveth the increase."

Such a spirit is lovely everywhere, but it is especially becoming in the minister of Christ. It is his high privilege to preach the Gospel, and he should seek to do it so as to hide himself. Standing in the halo round his Lord, men should not see him, but only the glory of the Saviour. They should "hear the voice, but see no man." Oh for more of the spirit of Daniel everywhere, but especially in the pulpits of the land!

Fourthly, we have here an illustration of faithful friendship. When Daniel was exalted, he did not forget his companions. Knit to Hananiah, Mishael, and Azariah by congenial tastes, as well as by the ties of country and religion, he had become to them a friend indeed; and they had shown their deep interest in and attachment to him, not only in sharing his protest against the diet of the college, but also in praying for him at his special request. It was meet, therefore, that he should remember them in his prosperity. He did no more than his duty toward them in speaking for their elevation, while, at the same time, he did a service to the king by introducing to him men of such integrity and ability.

But this conduct is not common; for many are like the chief butler, and in the hour of their exaltation forget the Joseph to whom, in their time of humiliation, they had been beholden. Multitudes are moved with envy, so that they cannot think of others rising; and even if they have been formerly indebted to them, they do their best to keep them down. But there was no such feeling in the breast of Daniel. The prosperity of his friends was his, and he would have them sharers with him in the honorable position to which their prayers had contributed to raise him. "A man that hath friends must show himself friendly ;" and there is a friend "that sticketh closer than a brother."

I cannot conclude without a word in reference to Daniel's greater Lord—Jesus Christ—of whom he prophesied. He, too, has been exalted. God has given him a name which is above every name. He is seated at the right hand of power—King of kings and Lord of lords—and in his exaltation all his people will share ; for it is written they shall "reign with him." Not, however, because they have been of service to him, as were his three friends to Daniel, but because he has "set his love upon them, and they have trusted in him." Let me ask you, my hearer, if there is a throne yonder for you? Do you love Jesus? Are you of his friends? Are you praying for the advancement of his cause and the coming of his kingdom? Are you working for his glory? Do you identify yourself with him? Are you one with him? Then for you there is a crown of righteousness, and a seat upon his throne. But if you repudiate his allegiance, and will have none of his love ; if you trample his grace underfoot, and insult his love by your base ingratitude—then will he destroy you as his enemies, and consign you to everlasting woe. Ah! why would you make him an enemy, when you may enjoy eternally the blessings of his friendship?

III.

THE DREAM RECOVERED AND INTER-PRETED.

DANIEL ii., 29-49.

THE vision which had so troubled Nebuchadnezzar was that of a huge image. It had a certain unity about it, inasmuch as it resembled a human figure. Yet it had also a strangely composite character, inasmuch as its different parts were made of different materials. The head was of gold, the breast and arms of silver, the belly and the thighs of brass, the legs of iron, and the feet part of iron and part of clay. But for all so stable as it seemed, the colossal figure was not destined to endure, for as the monarch gazed he saw severed, without hands, from its native rock, a stone, which smote the image and broke it in pieces. Then the stone itself gradually increased in size until it assumed the appearance of a mountain and filled the whole earth.

This huge image was by Daniel interpreted to mean what we may call the world-power. Its unity represents the fact that the different empires of earth are only parts of one great whole. They are all animated by the same spirit. They are all founded on human ambition. They are all antagonistic to God and to his truth. The body has many members, but all these members are moved by one will. So the successive world monarchies have all been pervaded by one spirit, which has striven through them to gain its own ends.

The separate parts of which the image was composed

were intended, according to Daniel's interpretation of them, to symbolize the characters of the different earthly empires, and the order in which they were to appear. The head of gold was the Babylonian monarchy of which Nebuchadnezzar was the king. It was the head, as the first in the order of time. It was of gold, as distinguished for the greatest magnificence. In Isaiah* Babylon is styled "the golden city;" elsewhere it is denominated by the same prophet "the glory of kingdoms, the beauty of the Chaldee's excellency;" "the lady of kingdoms;" while Jeremiah refers to it as "abundant in treasures," and as "the praise of the whole earth." Its kings had enriched its capital with the spoils of conquest, and adorned it with the products of other lands, as well as with works of art and gardens of beauty, so that it was regarded as one of the wonders of the world. Most appropriately, therefore, does Daniel say to Nebuchadnezzar, "Thou art this head of gold."

"The breast and the arms of silver" represent what is known in history as the Medo-Persian Empire, the foundation of which was laid by Cyrus when he conquered Babylon. It lasted for about two hundred years, and extended through the reigns of those kings who so frequently attempted the invasion of Greece, and whose defeats have given immortality to the names of Leonidas and Themistocles, and made Thermopylæ and Salamis renowned. It is said here to be inferior to the Babylonian kingdom, and this may refer either to the absence of that magnificence for which Nebuchadnezzar was famous, or to the degenerate character of the Persian rulers; for, as Prideaux† has said, with the exception of Cyrus himself, the kings of Persia

---

* Isa. xiii., 19; xiv., 4; xlvii., 5; Jer. li., 13, 41.
† "Connection of the History of the Old and New Testament," vol. i., p. 107.

were "the worst race of men that ever governed an empire." Or it may refer to the disastrous defeats sustained by the Persians in the military campaigns which they undertook. Their plans for conquest were foolishly contrived and madly carried out, so that they resulted frequently in inglorious failures. In this respect, therefore, there was an evident appropriateness in speaking of Persia as inferior to Babylon.

"The belly and the thighs of brass" represent the Grecian Empire, which rose to pre-eminence in the days of Alexander the Great, and which latterly assumed the form of two separate monarchies, the one in Syria under the descendants of Seleucus, and the other in Egypt under the Ptolemies. This kingdom is not inaptly symbolized by brass, inasmuch as the Greeks were famous for their brazen armor. It is declared that this third empire should "bear rule over all the earth," but the words must be taken somewhat hyperbolically. Alexander, indeed, commanded that he should be styled "the King of the Whole World;" but he had not really conquered the whole earth. Still, as he had authority over large territories in Europe, Asia, and Africa—that is to say, in all the divisions of the world then known—the description may be legitimately applied to him.

Hence all admit that this third empire is the Macedonian; but it has been disputed whether the kingdoms of the Seleucidæ and the Ptolemies are to be reckoned as in some sort a continuation of the Macedonian Empire, or are to be regarded as themselves constituting the fourth monarchy here symbolized by the legs of iron, and the feet part of iron and part of clay.

After careful examination, I have adopted the opinion that these two kingdoms are here viewed as constituting a continuation of the Macedonian Empire, for, as Dr. Pusey has remarked, "these two dynasties, ever at variance with

one another, had no unity; they were in no sense a kingdom, except as they were connected with the great empire-
plan of Alexander.   They were continuations of Greek pre-
dominance over the nations of Oriental character in Asia
Minor, Egypt, Syria, and Assyria.   They carried out that
interpenetration of the Greek and Oriental nations which
Alexander must have contemplated; they Hellenized Egypt
and Western Asia, and unknowingly prepared the way for
the Gospel by diffusing, through the means of their Greek
cities, the language in which it was to be given."* We regard, therefore, the belly and thighs of brass as symbolizing
the Macedonian Empire; first, one under Alexander, and
then ultimately branching into two main divisions under the
Seleucidæ in the north and the Ptolemies in the south.

"The legs of iron" represent the Roman power, which
was remarkable for nothing so much as for strength.   Its
legions carried everything before them, reducing independent kingdoms into conquered provinces, and holding the
proudest nations under the most galling tribute.   From
Parthia, in the East, to Gaul, and even to Britain, in the
West, its power extended, and everywhere it was a thing of
iron, crushing and breaking all that stood in its way.   But
in process of time, its strength was weakened by the admixt-
ure of inferior elements with its original population; so that
while the legs are of iron, the feet are part of iron and part
of potter's clay.   That which was, in one sense, the proof
of its greatness, became, in another, the precursor of its decay.   By its martial might Rome conquered many nations;
but the mingling of these diverse and degenerate peoples
with its noble citizenship deteriorated the empire as a whole,
and made it, in the end, an easy prey to the Northern hordes
of barbarians by whom it was ultimately overrun.   Every

---

* "Lectures on Daniel the Prophet," pp. 67, 68.

reader of Gibbon's history is familiar with this view of the
case, but we may be pardoned for reproducing this passage
from his pages in support of it :

"During the first four ages, the Romans in the laborious
school of poverty had acquired the virtues of war, and government by the vigorous exertion of those virtues ; and, by
the assistance of fortune, they had obtained, in the course
of the three succeeding centuries, an absolute empire over
many countries of Europe, Asia, and Africa. The last hundred years had been consumed in apparent prosperity and
internal decline. The nation of soldiers, magistrates, and
legislators who composed the thirty-five tribes of the Roman people was dissolved into the common mass of mankind, and confounded with the millions of servile provin-
cials who had received the name without imbibing the spirit
of Romans. A mercenary army, levied among the subjects
and barbarians of the frontier, was the only order of men
who preserved and abused their independence. By their
tumultuary election, a Syrian, a Goth, or an Arab was exalted to the throne, and invested with despotic powers over
the conquests and over the country of the Scipios. The
limits of the Roman Empire still extended from the Western Ocean to the Tigris, and from Mount Atlas to the Rhine
and Danube. To the undiscerning eye of the vulgar, Philip
appeared a monarch no less powerful than Hadrian or Augustus had formerly been. The form was still the same,
but the animating health and vigor were fled. The industry of the people was discouraged and exhausted by a long
series of oppressions. The discipline of the legions which
alone, after the extinction of every other virtue, had propped
the greatness of the State, was corrupted by ambition, or re-
laxed by the weakness of the emperors. The strength of
the frontiers, which had always consisted in arms rather
than in fortifications, was insensibly undermined, and the

fairest provinces were left exposed to the rapaciousness or ambition of the barbarians, who soon discovered the decline of the Roman Empire."*

The fourth kingdom, therefore, symbolized by the legs and feet of the image, was the Roman power, which, in its early days, was strong as iron, but in its later history had elements of weakness, as if the iron had been mixed with clay. The toes of the image, like the ten horns of the beast afterward seen by Daniel, are believed by some to represent the separate monarchies into which the Roman Empire came to be divided, and much learned ingenuity has been exerted by expositors in seeking to identify these ten kingdoms in modern Europe; but that is a branch of the investigation for which I have little relish, and I prefer to leave with you the general impression which I have made, rather than to confuse your minds by an enumeration which, after all, must be mainly conjectural.

We come now to the kingdom represented by the stone which destroyed the image. It will be at once apparent that this figure is intended to symbolize the kingdom of our Lord Jesus Christ; but the great question among modern interpreters is, whether the cutting-out of the stone from the mountain and its coming into collision with the image is to be understood of the first advent of Christ, which is already past, or of his second coming, which is yet future. Dr. Tregelles, who may be taken as speaking for the whole pre-millenarian school, says, "The falling of the stone on the image must mean destroying judgment on the fourth Gentile power, not gradual evangelization of it by grace; and the destroying judgment cannot be dealt by Christians, for they are taught to submit to the powers that be; so that it must be dealt by Christ himself at his coming again. We live

---

* Gibbon, chap. vii.   Quoted also by Barnes, "Commentary," *in loco.*

under the divisions of the Roman Empire which began fourteen hundred years ago, and which, at the time of his coming, shall be definitely ten. All that had failed in the hand of man shall then pass away, and that which is kept in his own hand shall be introduced."*

Now, it must be confessed that much may be said in favor of this view, and that it has, besides, a wonderful fascination for the devout soul that is distressed by the prevalence of evil in the world. In particular, it seems to harmonize with the statement that the stone came into collision with the feet of the image. If the reference be to the first coming of Christ, how, it may be asked, could Jesus be said to strike against a form of the Roman Empire which did not then exist? And how can the breaking in pieces of the image symbolize the peaceful character of his mission and the quiet progress of his cause?

But, in answer to the first of these inquiries, we may say, that as the world-power is here represented by one ideal image, whatever comes against any single portion of the image may be viewed as directed against it as a whole; and so the advent of Christ, though it came before the final division of the Roman Empire, may be regarded as coming into collision with the spirit by which every form of that empire was animated. Besides, the words "in the days of these kings" refer not to the kings of the Roman Empire alone, but to all the kings represented by this composite image, and the meaning is that some time during the history of those kings thus symbolized the God of heaven should set up his kingdom.

The second question may be answered by such a criticism on the thirty-fifth verse as that of Mr. Barnes, who

---

* "Remarks on the Prophetic Visions of the Book of Daniel," pp. 24, 25, by S. P. Tregelles. London: Baxter, 1852.

says : " The connection here and the whole statement would seem to demand the sense of a continued or prolonged smiting, or of repeated blows rather than a single concussion. The great image was not only thrown down, but there was a subsequent process of comminution independent of what would have been produced by the fall. A fall would only have broken it into large blocks or fragments, but this continued smiting reduced it to powder. This would imply, therefore, not only a single shock, but some cause continuing to operate until that which had been overthrown was effectually destroyed, like a vast image reduced to impalpable powder."*

But whether or not these explanations be satisfactory, there seems to me to be one fatal objection to the view of those who take the severing of the stone from the mountain to mean the second coming of Christ; for if that interpretation be correct, it will follow that the kingdom of the Messiah has not yet been founded on the earth. I know, indeed, that Dr. Tregelles and his school would draw a distinction between the kingdom of grace and the kingdom of glory, and would make the vision here refer to the setting-up of the kingdom of glory. But that does not mend the matter; for if that be true, then it will follow that in a vision given to Nebuchadnezzar with the view of making known to him what should be hereafter there is positively no allusion to the most important fact in the annals of humanity—the Incarnation—a fact, moreover, which was to have such a momentous bearing on the after-history of every nation on the earth. That the vision, altogether ignoring the first coming of Christ, should leap forward to his second advent, appears to me to be utterly inconceivable, the more especially as the phraseology here used by Daniel to describe the king-

---

* "Notes on Daniel," *in loco.*

dom of the stone is identical with that employed by Isaiah in predicting the birth of the Messiah: "Of the increase of his government and peace there shall be no end, upon the throne of David, and upon his kingdom, to order it, and to establish it with judgment and with justice from henceforth even forever;"* and also with that addressed by the angel to Mary at the Annunciation: "Thou shalt bring forth a son, and shalt call his name Jesus. He shall be great, and shall be called the Son of the Highest; and the Lord God shall give unto him the throne of his father David: and he shall reign over the house of Jacob forever; and of his kingdom there shall be no end."† Moreover, John the Baptist heralded the coming of the Redeemer in these words: "Repent ye, for the kingdom of heaven is at hand."‡ Jesus himself began his public ministry with this declaration: "The time is fulfilled, and the kingdom of God is at hand;"§ and throughout his career as an instructor he was continually uttering parables in illustration of "the kingdom of God" or "the kingdom of heaven." Nay, to such an extent did he dwell on the idea of his royalty that he was accused of setting himself up against Cæsar; and when Pilate asked him if he were a king, he did not repudiate the dignity, but only said, "My kingdom is not of this world."‖

We cannot, therefore, accept as correct any interpretation of this vision which requires us to believe that the kingdom of heaven has not yet been set up in the world, or which, in its eagerness to unfold what shall be when the Lord comes the second time, compels us to ignore the grace and the glory of his first appearance. Hence, other difficulties notwithstanding, I take the severance of the stone from the mountain to denote the coming of Christ into the world, and the

---

* Isa. ix., 7.   † Luke i., 31–33.   ‡ Matt. iii., 1.
§ Mark i., 15.   ‖ John xviii., 36.

collision of the stone with the image to mean the founding
by the Lord of that spiritual kingdom which is, in its principles, antagonistic to all the world-powers, and which will
ultimately subdue them all.   Thus viewed, the vision which
Daniel recovered and interpreted suggests to us many interesting things concerning the kingdom of Christ, which, however, I can dwell on but for a little season.

There is, in the first place, its superhuman origin.   The
stone was "cut out" of the mountain without hands.
There was no natural cause for its severance.   It did not
fall by its own weight, through the force of gravitation, or
by accident, for it was "cut."   And yet, the cutting was the
work of no ordinary agent, for it was cut "without hands."
So the foundation of Christ's kingdom was the result of no
development of human character, but rather of the bringing
of a new spiritual and heavenly power into the world.   Left
to itself, the world-power deteriorates, and that image whose
head is of gold has feet part of iron and part of clay.   That
is the sort of development of human character which is seen
in the history of the empires of earth.   If, therefore, the
Lord Jesus had been the product merely of his age, he could
not have risen above his age ; rather, following the law of
development which, in moral things at least, the human race,
left to itself, has always illustrated, he would have fallen below his age.   By the miraculous manner of his birth, however, and the mysterious constitution of his person as God
and man, in two distinct natures, the ordinary course and
chain of natural causes was broken in upon, and a new
and divine agency was brought to bear upon the kingdoms
of the earth.   But for this supernatural intervention, they
would have gone on unchecked, each rising into importance, and then falling to pieces through the workings of
its own inherent corruption, or through the rise of another
upon its ruins.   But now a corrective influence has come

into operation, and its very difference from all that went
before it is a proof of its superhuman origin. The stone is
striking, one after another, earthly institutions and organizations, and by-and-by the Divine influence which it represents will permeate all ranks and conditions and kingdoms
of men.

There is, in the second place, the comparative feebleness
of its beginning. The language of the vision indicates that
the stone grew from a small size until it became a huge
mountain. Frequently earthly kingdoms have had very in-
significant beginnings; but, usually, that which has given
them the last accession of greatness has been some mighty
movement of its armies or some grand achievement of its
statesmen. Thus, to take a recent instance, every one is
familiar with the almost contemptible sovereignty of the
first of the Hohenzollern dynasty; but when, a few years
ago, while yet he was laying siege to the first city on the
continent of Europe, the King of Prussia caused himself, in
the palace of a conquered monarch, to be proclaimed Emperor of Germany, the pomp and ceremony of the occasion
were so great that the correspondent of the leading English
journal finished his description of the event with these high-
sounding words, "This will live in history." That is how
empires are founded among men.

But let that be contrasted with the meeting of a few Gali-
lean peasants in an upper room, surrounding a Teacher who,
within a few hours, was to be ruthlessly dragged from their
fellowship and nailed to a cross. Hear him saying unto
them, "I appoint unto you a kingdom, as my Father hath
appointed unto me; that ye may eat and drink at my table
in my kingdom, and sit on thrones judging the twelve tribes
of Israel,"* and you have a vivid idea of the circumstances

---

* Luke xxii., 29.

in which the proclamation of the "kingdom of heaven" was made. Poor, despised, contemptible to human view, its subjects were — too contemptible at first almost to be persecuted, but destined in the end to overcome the world by the weapon of their love.

Behold that little Jewish-looking man of weak bodily presence, stepping ashore from the boat which has just come to the harbor of Neapolis from Troas. He is accompanied by a travelling doctor and a quiet youth. He asks some one on the pier to show him the way to Philippi, and then he sets out in the direction indicated to him. Who is he? What is he going to do? Surely he is nobody of much importance, and cannot have any great work in charge! So we might judge, according to appearance. Yet it is the apostle Paul, bringing with him the Gospel to Europe, and going to found Christ's kingdom in the classic land of Greece. A few days after this, two of these men were in prison; and yet, ere they were fixed in the stocks, they had already smitten the world-image, for in their healing of the Pythoness and in the conversion of Lydia the evil power of the world had received the first of that series of blows which it has been receiving at intervals ever since, and which ere long shall crush it until it shall become like "the chaff of the summer threshing-floors."

There is, in the third place, the gradualness of its progress. The stone grew until it became a mountain. Not all at once was this development made. It was a work of time. And so in the kingdom which it symbolizes advancement was by degrees. Beginning at Jerusalem, its first preachers sought their earliest converts among their fellow-countrymen; but as the seed sloughs off its outward shell when it begins to grow, the Christian Church very soon put off its Jewish restrictiveness and found a root in Gentile cities.

We see, in the Acts of the Apostles, how, from one centre of influence to another, Paul went on and up, until at length he made his way to Rome, and had his converts both in the "palace of the Cæsars" and in the legions of the Empire. Then, within a few centuries, it overspread Europe; and though during the mediæval times it seemed to be standing still, it put forth new energy at the era of the Reformation. Since that date it has gone on advancing; but probably the most rapid strides have been taken by it during the years of the present· century. Almost within the limits of two generations, the Bible has been translated into two hundred different languages, and missionaries have gone to the East and to the West, to the North and to the South, and have in many instances created a new civilization by their efforts. Every month, almost, is bringing fresh evidences of their success; and within the last few days I have heard tidings from Japan which have filled my heart with joy. Two years ago I told from this pulpit the story of Joseph Nee Sima,* who ran away from Japan in his eagerness to learn, and came, in the wondrous providence of God, to this country, where he became a Christian, and was educated as a missionary. He left a few months ago for his native land, and in the *Missionary Herald* for March† there is a letter describing his welcome in his father's house. His parents and friends have renounced idolatry; and he writes, "Besides my home friends, my humble labor within three weeks in this place has been wonderfully blessed. I have preached several times in a school-house in this town, and also to small audiences in different families. A week before last Sabbath I preached to a large audience in a Buddhist temple. All the priests in this community came and listened

---

* See "David, King of Israel," pp. 128, 129.

† In the year 1875.

to the preaching of the new religion." "Is not my word a fire, saith the Lord, and a hammer that breaketh the rock in pieces?" Here is another smiting process going on. The mountain is increasing; for this is but a specimen of what is going on in many lands; and soon the oracle of Isaiah will be fulfilled: "The mountain of the Lord's house shall be established on the top of the mountains, and all nations shall flow unto it."

There is, fourthly, its universal extent. The mountain "filled the whole earth." "The knowledge of the Lord shall cover the earth." There are few things more clearly revealed in prophecy than this. Again and again is it declared that "all the ends of the earth shall remember and turn unto the Lord, and all the kindreds of the nations do homage before him." To the superficial observer, indeed, it may seem as if this were the most visionary idea that ever entered the mind of man; but when he takes a broader and deeper view, he may see reason to alter his opinion.

Astronomers calculate the orbit and period of a planet by taking observations of it at different and distant intervals, and from the comparison of these they can predict with unerring accuracy both its course and its reappearance. Now, if we will take our estimate of the future history of the kingdom of Christ on similar principles, we shall be led to regard the universal diffusion of the Gospel as among the most certain of future events. Let your first observation be in the days of Paul, your second in the time of Constantine, your third in the era of the Reformers, your fourth in the generation of the Wesleys and the Whitefields, and your fifth at the present hour, and you will be led to conclude that if only the churches of Christ will do their duty aright, we are not so very far from the universal triumph of the Gospel.

I saw in an English newspaper, the other day, that a

grain of wheat, which, five years ago, had been picked up by an admirer of royalty as it fell from the hand of the Prince of Wales, had, by being sown, produced, in that short interval, as much as could be drilled into sixteen acres of land. And if we would only catch as eagerly, and sow as diligently, the seed that falls from the hand of the Prince of Peace, we might soon be able with the increase to cover the whole earth. "There shall be a handful of corn in the earth on the top of the mountains; the fruit thereof shall shake like Lebanon." Ah! if we but prized our privilege as fellow-workers with God in this matter, we should be found more fervent in our prayers, more diligent in our labors, and more liberal in our gifts, for this great cause.

There is, fifthly, the perpetual duration of this kingdom. "It shall never be destroyed;" and "it shall not be left to other people." "No weapon that is formed against it shall prosper; and every tongue that riseth up in judgment against it God will condemn." Often the kings of the earth have set themselves, and the rulers have taken counsel together, against it, and sometimes it has almost seemed as if they had destroyed it; but still, like its great Lord, it has come forth with new power and majesty from the grave in which they dreamed it had been buried, and gone forth to grander triumphs than ever before. All the cruelties that ingenuity could devise, and all the efforts that earthly power could put forth, have been tried against it. Men have set up gibbets and stakes for the destruction of those who were laboring for its advancement, but in vain. It has in it the immortality of its Lord. Earthly might can only overthrow that which is like unto itself. An army may destroy an army, but by what external power can you annihilate love? You may kill the man, but you cannot kill the principle. Phœnix-like, that will ever rise again from the ashes of the martyr; and the persecutor, though to superficial eyes he

seems the victor, does only in reality own himself the vanquished.   Thus the perpetuity of this kingdom is intimately associated with its character, and that again with its
origin.

Probably no one ever knew more of what imperial power
could effect than did the First Napoleon, and so his testimony may be of value here.   " I know men," said he, in conversation with General Bertrand, " and Jesus Christ is not a
man.   Superficial minds see a resemblance between Christ
and the founder of empires and the gods of other religions.
That resemblance does not exist.   There is between Christ
and all other religions whatsoever the distance of infinity ;
from the first day to the last, he is the same—always the
same, majestic and simple, infinitely firm and infinitely gen-
tle."   And then he goes on to contrast him with Alexander, with Cæsar, and with himself, in that they founded their
empires on power, but he on love.   The emperor was right ;
and in that difference lies the hope of the world, for love is
a principle which is simply indestructible, and the self-sacri-
fice of the cross demonstrates the perpetuity of the throne.

IV.

THE NON-CONFORMISTS OF BABYLON.

DANIEL iii.

AFTER the recovery and interpretation of his dream by Daniel, Nebuchadnezzar appears to have been deeply impressed with the greatness of that God to whose revelation of the secret the young captive ascribed his success. But these feelings soon subsided. They were "as a morning cloud and as the early dew;" for the next time we hear of him in the prophet's narrative is in connection with a magnificent religious festival, which he held at the inauguration of a colossal idol, reared by him in honor of his favorite divinity, Bel-Merodach.

Nor need we be surprised at this, as if it were at all uncommon among ourselves. Who has not known a history like this? By some signal providence, or in some unmistakable manner, Jehovah has confronted a careless man, who, startled by the discovery at once of his own littleness and of God's majesty, has been profoundly moved. Sudden as a lightning-flash in the night season, the conviction of the dread reality and importance of eternity has shot through his soul. He speaks on these momentous matters as he never did before. He seeks to honor God's ministers by every means in his power. In one word, he seems, to the merely human onlooker, to be thoroughly converted. But after a while, the impressions which appeared to be so deep are effaced, and he is seen rearing a huge image, not necessarily in the shape of a golden statue, but in the form of some glory, or greatness, or pleasure before which he bows himself, and at whose shrine he expects that others also will do homage.

Let us beware, therefore, lest, in condemning the Babylonian monarch here, we be not at the same time pronouncing sentence upon ourselves. We profess to believe in and honor the God and Father of our Lord Jesus Christ; we ascribe to him in words "the greatness, and the power, and the glory, and the victory, and the majesty;" we add our "Amen" to the Doxology, which says, "To him be glory and dominion." But is there no golden image that has our real allegiance? Are we not prone to raise even above Jehovah our success in business, or our pre-eminence in society, or our position in the State, or our place in the estimation of our fellow-men? Are we not all too apt to reckon these things, or things like these, the objects of our chief interest, the ends for which we labor; yea, the ambitions in our intense devotion to which we are wearing out our lives "in a melancholy and thankless martyrdom?" While, therefore, we are thoroughly alive to the sin of Nebuchadnezzar here, let us search and see that no similar idol has a place in our hearts or in our homes, in our counting-rooms or in our stores, in our churches or in our pulpits.

The date of the erection of this image by Nebuchadnezzar is not mentioned in the record; but some have supposed that several years elapsed between the events narrated in the second chapter and those now introduced to the reader Prideaux* places the holding of this high festival after Nebuchadnezzar's return from the destruction of Jerusalem with the blinded Zedekiah among his captives; and it is by no means improbable that he meant on that special occasion to exalt his god above the Jehovah of the Hebrews.

---

* "Connection of the History of the Old and New Testament," vol. i., p. 82.

The image was of gold. If this means that it was composed of a solid mass of the precious metal, then an enormous amount of treasure must have been required for its construction. Still, taking the resources of the empire into consideration, there is no impossibility involved even in that view of the case. But as the very terms here employed are elsewhere used to denote that which was simply overlaid with gold,* we may conclude that this immense image was formed of wood covered with a thin layer of gold.

Its height was sixty cubits and its breadth six cubits ; but as the length of the cubit is uncertain, it is impossible to determine with accuracy what these figures would represent in feet and inches. The proportion of the height to the breadth is as ten to one ; but as the usual ratio in the case of the human figure is that of six to one, it is conjectured that the number sixty here includes the height of the pedestal as well as that of the image, properly so called.

The idol was set up in the plain of Dura, which, as it is said to belong to the province of Babylon, must be sought for in the neighborhood of the city. For this reason I cannot accept the view of those who would identify it with the place called Dur, on the left bank of the Tigris, and one hundred and twenty miles from Babylon. More probable is the opinion of Oppert, who thinks he has found the scene of this festival in the vicinity of the mound of Dowair, or Duair, where also he discovered the pedestal of a colossal statue.†

To the inauguration of this great image Nebuchadnezzar summoned representatives from all the provinces of his empire, in the persons of those who held high office under him.

---

* See Pusey's "Lectures on Daniel the Prophet," p. 445, note ; also Fairbairn's "Dictionary," article NEBUCHADNEZZAR ; Exod. xxx., 1, 3 ; xxxix., 38.

† Smith's "Dictionary," *sub voce.*

Much ingenious antiquarian research has been expended on
the investigation of the particular grade of office denoted
by each term employed in the second and third verses of
this chapter; but it would serve no good purpose to enter
upon such a subject here. Let it be merely remarked that
it was the Babylonian custom to leave over each conquered
province a prince belonging to the vanquished nation, while
they and the peoples whom they governed were brought under tribute to the empire. Thus even after the captivity of
Judah, the rulers of that province were Jews, most of whom
belonged to the royal family, though some of them were of
inferior rank. Now, this peculiarity in the nationality of
these officials will, I think, give us an insight into the motive of Nebuchadnezzar in bringing them together at this
time, and commanding them to worship the image which he
had set up. He wished to assert his sovereignty over them,
and, through them, over all his subjects in the most absolute
manner. He knew, moreover, that nothing so contributes
to the perpetuation of nationality, and the desire for independence in a conquered province, as the maintenance of
its old historic religion, hallowed to the people by the associations of the past. So, wishing to weld the many kingdoms of his empire into one homogeneous whole, he determined to ask from them all conformity to the idol-worship
which he himself preferred. No doubt, therefore, this religious service had a political design. It was not merely
his enthusiasm for his god, though that was great, that im-
pelled Nebuchadnezzar to make the decree which gathered
all his subordinates to the plain of Dura. His religious fervor, as in the case of multitudes since his day, was subordi-
nated to imperial policy; and unity of worship was sought
only that it might contribute to the political unity of the
empire.

Some, indeed, have thought that the image here set up

was designed to symbolize the monarch himself; and it is beyond doubt that among the Persians, as in later days among the Romans, the emperor was invested with a sort of quasi-divinity; but it is more in harmony with what we know of Nebuchadnezzar from other sources to suppose that he intended this idol to represent Bel-Merodach. Mr. Rawlinson, whose brother has earned for himself a world-wide reputation in connection with the deciphering of the cuneiform inscriptions on the Assyrian monuments, thus speaks of the description given in these old stone books of this king: "We can only observe as peculiar to Nebuchad-nezzar a disposition to rest his fame on his great works rather than on his military achievements; and a strong re-ligious spirit manifesting itself especially in a direction which is almost exclusive to one particular god. Though his own tutelary deity and that of his father was Nebo (Mer-cury), yet his worship, his ascriptions of praise, his thanks-givings, have in almost every case for their object the god Merodach. Under his protection he placed his son Evil-Merodach. Merodach is 'his lord;' his 'great lord;' the 'joy of his heart;' the great lord who has appointed him to the empire of the world, and has confided to his care the far-spread people of the earth; the great lord who has estab-lished him in strength, etc. One of the first of his own titles is, 'he who pays homage to Merodach.' Even when restor-ing the temples of other deities, he ascribes the work to the suggestion of Merodach, and places it under his protection. We may hence explain the appearance of a sort of mono-theism mixed with polytheism in the Scriptural notices of him. While admitting a qualified divinity in Nebo, Nana, and other deities of his country, he maintained the real monarchy of Bel-Merodach. He was to him 'the supreme chief of the gods;' the most ancient, the king of the heav-ens and the earth. It was his image or symbol undoubtedly which was set up in the plain of Dura, and his house in which the sacred vessels of the Temple were treasured. He seems at some times to have identified this his supreme god with the God of the Jews, and at other times to have regarded the Jewish God as one of the local and inferior divinities over whom Merodach ruled."*

Thus, his religious proselytism combined with his political ambition to stimulate him to convoke this great assembly, and to call on every one present at it to worship the image which he had set up.

The signal for the worshipping of this huge idol was to be given by the sounds of music. Over the names of these instruments in the original, great learned warfare has been waged, and much ink has been shed. Some of them, it has been alleged, are of Greek origin; and, as the Greek language was not known at that early date in Babylon, it follows—so objectors reason—that the Book of Daniel, in which these terms are found, could not have been written until the times of the Maccabees, when Greek words and Greek instruments were well known among the Jews. The answers to this argument may be seen at large in Dr. Pusey's "Lectures on Daniel the Prophet."† I content myself now with giving you the gist of the matter in the following sentences: "Asia, from the Tigris westward, was systematically intersected with lines of commerce. Sardis and Babylon were professedly luxurious. It were rather a marvel if the golden, music-loving city had not gathered to itself foreign musical instruments of all sorts, or if, in a religious inauguration at Babylon, all the variety of music which it could command had not been united to grace the festival and bear along the minds and imaginations of the people. The Greek

---

* Smith's "Dictionary," article NEBUCHADNEZZAR.
† Pusey's "Lectures on Daniel the Prophet," pp. 24-33.

names are but another instance of the old recognized fact that the name of an import travels with the thing. There is nothing stranger in our finding Greek instruments of music in Nebuchadnezzar's time at Babylon than in the Indian names of Indian animals and of an Indian tree having reached Jerusalem under Solomon."*

When these musical instruments were sounded, there was to be a universal prostration before the image; and if any one refused to render this homage, he was "in the same hour" to be cast into a burning fiery furnace. This was a punishment distinctively Babylonian, just as the placing of men in the dens of wild animals was a cruelty distinctively Persian; and so, in the nature of the penalty here denounced against disobedience we have an incidental corroboration of the authenticity of the history. We know nothing of the sort of furnace that is here referred to, and cannot tell whether it had any resemblance to our modern smelting fires. As its intensity could be increased by the employment of certain means not here specified, it would seem to have been enclosed in some way; as four persons could walk to and fro in it, we conclude that it must have been of immense size; and as these persons could be seen in it by spectators who were far enough away from it to be beyond the reach of harm from it, we infer that it must have been so placed as to be open to the inspection of persons at a distance. It was a fearful thing to face; but even with this dreadful fate before them, there were some who had the courage to refuse obedience to the king's command. Daniel's three friends, Hananiah, Mishael, and Azariah, would not bow the knee to the image which the king had erected. They were willing, in all civil things, to be good, law-abiding subjects of Nebuchadnezzar; but in a matter of this sort,

---

* Pusey's "Lectures on Daniel the Prophet," pp. 26, 27.

they felt that they owed allegiance to a higher King, who had said to them, " Thou shalt have no other gods before me. Thou shalt not make unto thee any graven image, or any likeness of anything that is in heaven above, or that is in the earth beneath, or that is in the water under the earth : thou shalt not bow down thyself to them, nor serve them ;"* and so, without making any great demonstration of their procedure, they simply refrained from doing as the king required.

But keen-eyed Envy was closely watching how they would conduct themselves. Their rapid elevation to posts of honor and emolument, over the heads of many older men, had made them many enemies. When, therefore, it was observed that they did not fall down and worship the image, certain of the Chaldeans, moved with jealousy, and forgetful of the fact that they themselves had owed their lives on a former occasion to the interposition of Daniel and his friends, informed the monarch of their contumacy.

When he heard their report, Nebuchadnezzar was enraged. Here was a defying of his authority by those who, he perhaps imagined, owed more to him than many others, and so their disobedience might wear, in his eyes, the color of ingratitude. But he would not be in haste. He would give them another opportunity to consider their position before he consigned them to the fire. Hence he closely questioned them, and issued anew the command that at the appointed signal they should prostrate themselves before the image, saying also, in the haughtiness of his heart, " If ye fall down and worship the image which I have made, well : but if ye worship not, ye shall be cast the same hour into the midst of a burning fiery furnace ; and who is that God that shall deliver you out of my hands ?"

---

* Exod. xx., 3-5.

But they were still unmoved, and said, in the strength of their faith, "We are not careful to answer thee in this matter. If it be so, our God whom we serve is able to deliver us from the burning fiery furnace, and he will deliver us out of thine hand, O King. But if not, be it known unto thee, O King, that we will not serve thy gods, nor worship the golden image which thou hast set up."

This answer, so calm, so dignified, so courageous, filled the monarch with such rage that he commanded that the furnace should be heated seven times more than it was wont to be heated, and after the three young men had been bound, he ordered that they should be cast into the fire, the heat of which was so great that the men who flung them into the furnace were themselves consumed.

And now it might have been thought that there was an end of the matter; but no! for as the king looked on he saw the three men begin to move about in the furnace, accompanied by a fourth, whose aspect was so heavenly that he seemed to him to be like a "son of the gods." The singularity of the spectacle filled Nebuchadnezzar with astonishment and dismay; and going as near as he could to the mouth of the furnace, he cried, "Shadrach, Meshach, and Abednego, ye servants of the most high God, come forth and come hither;" and they came forth unharmed, for the fire had no power over their bodies, "nor was an hair of their head singed, neither were their coats changed, nor had the smell of fire passed upon them."

And who was this mysterious one, the fourth in the fire, to whom, as it would seem, they owed their deliverance? Nebuchadnezzar, describing him, says, "The form of the fourth is like the son of God." Now, this language would almost make it appear that the king knew something of the Messiah who is called in the Old Testament sometimes by this name; but when we give the literal translation, "the

form of the fourth is like a son of the gods," we see that he
was speaking like a heathen, and meant only to describe
the dignified and exalted deportment of him whom he thus
characterized.

Still, though the Babylonian monarch had no conception
of the Messiah, and, indeed, thought of this person (as we
see in verse twenty-eight) as an angel, we have no doubt
whatever that he was "the angel of the covenant," of whom
we so often read in the Hebrew Scriptures, and whose ap-
pearances were in reality so many anticipations of the Incarnation in the person of Christ. He with whom Abraham pleaded for guilty Sodom, and with whom Jacob wres-
tled at Peniel till the dawning of the day; he whose fiery
glory filled the bush without consuming it as Moses turned
aside to see the sight; he who appeared to Joshua as the
captain of the host of the Lord, and to Manoah and his
wife as the wonderful one; he who spoke to Gideon at the
wine-press of Ophrah, and to David at the threshing-floor
of Araunah, was the same great and gracious one who
walked in the furnace with his persecuted servants here,
and was the second person of the glorious Trinity. To
him, therefore, to whom we are beholden for our great salvation, these Hebrew non-conformists were indebted for
their miraculous deliverance, and so the king was not wrong
in ascribing to him the glory of their safety; though he is
not to be commended in the fact that he sought to enforce
the duty of reverencing the name of Jehovah by civil pains
and penalties, not less reprehensible in kind, though less
cruel in degree, than those which he had denounced on such
as would not worship his image.

But where was Daniel all this while? Some have supposed that he was present, and was one of those who refused to bow the knee to the idol, but that his enemies,
knowing his position with the monarch, feared to bring

an accusation against him first, and so began with his three friends, reserving him for a subsequent attack. But. I cannot accept that explanation. Daniel was altogether too noble a man and too chivalrous a friend to seek to escape in such a way. I am confident that if he had been present, he would at once have taken his place beside his former companions, and identified himself with their cause. Hence I rather believe that he was absent from Babylon at this time on some business of importance, and so was prevented from bearing testimony with his fellow-students to the unity and spirituality of God, and standing out against the sin of idolatry. Perhaps, too, his absence may help to account for the forwardness of the Chaldeans to present their impeachment. But however we may account for the silence of the record regarding him, we may be altogether certain that there was no trimming about him, and that no stain of dishonor rested on him for his non-appearance at this time. He was not the man to be ashamed of his Lord.

And now, passing from the mere exposition of the narrative, let us read its lessons in the light of modern life.

We have here, in the first place, a specimen of religious intolerance. God alone is "Lord of the conscience." A man's faith and worship are things which lie between himself and his Creator. What I shall believe concerning God, and how I shall worship God, no man may presume to determine for me. These are matters for myself alone; and no one, whether friend or foe, whether priest or king, has any authority in that domain. This liberty is my birthright as a man. My conscience is my glory; and to enslave that, if it were possible, would make me ten thousand times more a bondman than to chain me to the galley, or to consign me to weary drudgery under some task-master's eye. The latter is the slavery of the body; the former is an inthralment of the soul. Therefore all arguments that tell against slave-holding tell with increased power against religious intolerance. But to the Christian it wears also a sacrilegious aspect. He regards himself as "not his own." He keeps his conscience, therefore, for Christ. Hence religious intolerance is to him not only an interference with individual liberty, but also an infringement of the right of Christ to the absolute sovereignty of his soul. No doubt it may be said that Christians are commanded to be "subject to the higher powers;" and they are told that "whosoever resisteth the power, resisteth the ordinance of God." But we must interpret the precept of the Apostles by their practice. Now we find Peter saying before the Jewish rulers, "We ought to obey God rather than man;" and we know that Paul at last endured a martyr's death, because he would not, at the bidding of the Roman Emperor, abjure the Lord Jesus as his Redeemer and King.

These precepts which I have quoted from the apostolic epistles have respect to civil things, for which alone civil government was instituted, and in which alone it can find its legitimate province. In the matter of religion, the State has no authority, and it ought, therefore, to leave every man to his own conscience. The kingdoms and communities of the world have been long in learning these principles; and there is hardly a nation or even a religious denomination now existing which has not at some point in its past history been guilty of practising, or of advocating, persecution for the holding of some peculiar religious opinions. The Protestants may not imagine that Roman Catholics alone have indulged in it; nor are the hands of the Puritans themselves clean in this matter. But now let us hope that we are entering upon a new epoch; and as we execrate here the tyranny of Nebuchadnezzar, let us resolve that we shall never be parties to the attempt, by whomsoever made, to coerce the consciences of men by denouncing civil pains and penalties upon them for the holding of certain religious beliefs.

But, in the second place, we see here how religious intolerance is to be met. These three young men simply refused to do what Nebuchadnezzar commanded ; or, in modern phrase, they met his injunction with "passive resistance." The clear issue raised in their minds was this, "God says one thing, but Nebuchadnezzar says another: which shall we obey?" And they could not hesitate a moment for a reply. Some might have said to them, "You make too much of it; here is only a question of loyalty to the king. Your bowing before the image is not understood as an act of worship to it, but as an act of honor and obedience to the monarch. And surely, after all he has done for you, it will be ungracious to refuse that." But they would not tolerate any such casuistry. Nebuchadnezzar already knew their loyalty. They had shown that in more substantial ways to him. But this thing was simply and only idolatry, and they would not dishonor God in order to be loyal to the King of Babylon. They did not attack his position. They simply said "No" to him, and they said it as if they meant to abide by it.

Now, with similar firmness and humility we should meet intolerance yet. It has often been debated whether on religious grounds alone subjects or citizens would be warranted in taking up arms against the government of a country; and with the cases of the English Puritans and Scottish Covenanters before my mind, I will not undertake to decide it one way or other. But there is no such difficulty about passive resistance. That is always justifiable ; nay, it is always demanded of us when conscience is outraged, if, at least, we would not be guilty of high treason against him who is our rightful Lord.

The noble spirits who composed the Society of Friends

were among the earliest in more modern times to understand the meaning of "liberty of conscience," and to vindicate it, not only for themselves, but also for those who dif-
fered from them. Their great instrument was passive resistance, and working on with that, they became the pio-
neers of progress in the march of the nations toward perfect
religious freedom. We may smile occasionally at the oddity
of their dress or at the quaintness of their speech ; we may
think, too, that they carry some of their principles a shade
too far. But they have taught us all what liberty of conscience means ; and by their quiet bearing, as they refused
obedience to odious commands, they have shown us how intolerance is to be met. Let us give honor to the broad-brim
for this ; and in these days, when a British statesman has
dealt a crushing blow to the arrogant pretensions of the Vat-
ican, and eloquently defined the boundary between civil allegiance and loyalty to conscience, let us not forget the early
martyrs, to whom, in this matter, we are all indebted—men

> " Who lived unknown till persecution
> Chased them into fame, and dragged them
> Up to heaven ; whose blood was shed
> In confirmation of the noblest claim—
> Our claim to feed upon immortal truth,
> To soar, and to anticipate the skies."

We have here, thirdly, an illustration of the support which
Jesus gives to his followers, when they are called to suffer
for his sake. These three young men were entirely delivered, even as Peter was taken out of the prison at a later
day. But God's servants are not always brought out thus
from their tribulations. Still, they are always supported
through them. What is the martyrology of the Church but
just a commentary on these words, " My grace is sufficient
for thee ; my strength is made perfect in weakness ?" From
the days when Paul and Silas sung at midnight in the prison at Philippi, down to those when the Christians in Mada-

gascar met in the woods, and sung their hymns in whispers, lest their enemies might hear, we have a long series of instances, all tending to show that God is with his people in the furnace and supports them through it. If we may not say that he has always delivered them from their enemies, we can say that he has always advanced his kingdom in and through their sufferings. To such an extent has this been the case that the words of Tertullian have passed into a proverb: "The blood of the martyrs is the seed of the Church."

You have sometimes seen that the death of a Christian has, through his calm, quiet faith and hopeful, loving words, brought life to the souls of those who stood around his bed. So the deaths of the martyrs drew men's attention to the truth, for holding which they died. The very flames which burned them unbound their testimony, and sent it over the world, to tell of Jesus and his grace.

What the historian of the Scottish Reformation says about its protomartyr, Patrick Hamilton — namely, that "the smoke of his burning infected all on whom it blew" —is true of every martyrdom in some measure. It is thus bad policy in a civil government to persecute for religious opinions. It is what Talleyrand said is worse than a crime —a blunder. For if the victim believe error, then persecution gives him and his cause an importance which would not otherwise belong to it; and if he believe the truth, no human power can overthrow that, for it is immortal with the immortality of God.

But, in the fourth place, we see here that, in the matter of religious intolerance, as well as in some other things, the opposite of wrong is not always right. Nebuchadnezzar gave up the attempt to coerce these three valiant men. That was well; but he issued an edict in reference to Jehovah which had in it elements not less objectionable than his command to worship the image or his threat to put the disobedient into the furnace of fire. He had no more right to cut men in pieces for speaking evil of Jehovah than he had to put Shadrach and his companions into the flames for not worshipping his image. Both edicts were alike unjustifiable; and, as the subject has come thus incidentally before us, we may take advantage of the opportunity for bringing into prominence the great principles on which religious liberty rests, and in the maintenance of which it is to be preserved.

They are these four: first, that every citizen shall have perfect liberty to worship God according to his conscience; second, that the State shall protect every citizen in the enjoyment of that liberty so far as it does not interfere with the rights and liberties of others; third, that no citizen shall, in civil matters, be subjected to any disability on the ground of his religious belief; fourth, that no citizen shall have, in civil things, a preference given to him on the ground of his religious profession or belief.

It is in relation to the last of these that the danger of the present lies. That is the outermost bastion, which has been thrown up for the defence of the great citadel of freedom. There the first onslaught will be made, if it should ever be again attacked. There, therefore, let us be specially on our guard. Let us accept nothing for ourselves which we are not willing to give fully to others; and let us see to it that others are not buttressed and strengthened by the State simply and only on the ground of their religious creed. In one word, let us insist that the executive of the State shall confine itself to civil matters, and treat all religious denominations with neutrality by letting them all severely alone. All colors are alike in the dark; and all creeds will be alike to the State when, and only when, no church receives a single penny of its funds for any purpose whatsoever, and no citizen receives a boon of any sort simply and only for his religious creed.

V.

PRIDE ABASED.

DANIEL iv.

THE fourth chapter of the Book of Daniel consists of a decree published by Nebuchadnezzar, after he had passed through a series of most remarkable experiences; and we may, perhaps, have the clearest idea of its meaning and design, if we weave into a consecutive narrative the different incidents to which it refers.

After this Babylonian monarch had finished his military career by conquering all his enemies, he set himself to improve his territory, and beautify his capital with all the resources which he had accumulated. Whatever wealth could procure, or skill devise, or labor accomplish, was obtained by him for his country and his metropolis, until, at length, Babylon was ranked among the wonders of the world. Much had been done for that ancient city by Ninus and Semiramis, and even before the days of Nebuchadnezzar it was numbered among the grandest places on the surface of the earth; yet what the Rome of Augustus was to the Rome of the Republic, or what Paris under the last Napoleon was to Paris in the days of the first Revolution, that, only perhaps on a larger and more gorgeous scale, was Babylon under Nebuchadnezzar to Babylon as it existed before his days.

That we may see the truth of this statement, let us take a description of the city in its greatest splendor, and then mark how much of it is traced by ancient writers to the monarch of whom we speak.

The city stood on the river Euphrates, by which it is divided into two parts, Eastern and Western, and these were connected by a bridge of wonderful construction. "The wall was at least sixty miles in circumference, and would, of course, include an area three times as large as that covered by London and its appendages. It was laid out in six hundred and twenty-five squares, formed by the intersection of twenty-five streets at right angles. The walls, which were of brick, were at least seventy-five feet high and thirty-two broad. A trench surrounded the city, the sides of which were lined with brick and water-proof cement."* Now, the Eastern, or older, part of the city Nebuchadnezzar repaired and beautified throughout; the Western portion he added entirely himself; and the bridge which connected the two was of his construction. Besides these, he surrounded the entire city with several new lines of fortification, and constructed a new palace adjoining the old residence of his father. In the grounds of his palace he erected those hanging-gardens which were the marvel of the ancient world. His wife, having been brought up in Media, desired something to remind her of her native land; and for her satisfaction he constructed a raised terrace, on the summit of which were flowers and pleasure-grounds of the most beautiful description. This terrace is described as having been a square four hundred feet each way, and raised to an elevation of seventy-five feet above the ground. It was approached by sloping walks, and supported by a series of arched galleries increasing in height from the base to the summit. In these galleries were various chambers, one of which contained the engines by which water was raised from the river to the surface of the mound.

Nor are we dependent on the testimony of ancient histo-

---

* Eadie's "Cyclopædia," article BABYLON.

rians alone for these particulars. The Standard Inscription, referred to in my last discourse, relates at length the construction of the whole series of works, and appears to have been the authority from which Berosus drew; while the ruins of Babylon at this date, covering as they do an area of two hundred square miles, confirm this in the most decisive manner, for nine-tenths of the bricks found there are stamped with Nebuchadnezzar's name.

But his buildings were not confined to the city of Babylon. "I have examined," says Sir Henry Rawlinson, "the bricks *in situ* belonging, perhaps, to a hundred different towns and cities in the neighborhood of Bagdad, and I never found any other legend than that of Nebuchadnezzar, son of Nabopolassar, King of Babylon." Hence we may believe that throughout his empire he built or rebuilt cities, repaired temples, constructed quays, reservoirs, canals, and aqueducts on a scale of grandeur and magnificence surpassing everything of the kind recorded in history, unless it be the public works of one or two of the greatest Egyptian monarchs. There is also reason to conclude that an extensive system of irrigation was devised by him, and that the Babylonians were indebted to him for the vast net-work of canals which covered the whole alluvial tract between the two rivers (Tigris and Euphrates), and extended on the right bank of the Euphrates to the extreme verge of the stony desert.*

After all this building activity, and with a large amount of self-satisfaction at the completion of so many of his plans, the king was at rest in his palace, when a dream came to him in the visions of the night which made him sore afraid. As on the former occasion, he sent for the Chaldeans, and asked them to interpret it after he had told them what it was; for this time the thing had so deeply

---

* Smith's "Dictionary," article NEBUCHADNEZZAR.

burned itself upon his brain that he had not been able to forget it, and did not, therefore, need that it should be reproduced.

The vision was on this wise. He saw in the midst of the earth a tree, which grew so great that its height reached unto the heavens, and it was a conspicuous object even to the uttermost bound of the horizon. Its leaves were fair, and its fruit abundant. It gave shelter to the beasts of the field which gathered underneath its spreading boughs, and to the fowls of the air which built their nests in its leafy branches, and it afforded food to all who dwelt in its vicinity. At length, however, an angelic being made his appearance, and gave commandment that it should be hewn down, yet not so that it should be entirely destroyed, for its root was to be left in the earth. But at this stage of his injunction, the angel's language ceases to be applicable to a tree, and becomes such as could be fulfilled only in the case of a man : " Let his heart be changed from a man's, and let a beast's heart be given unto him ; and let seven times pass over him. This matter is by the decree of the watchers, and the demand by the word of the holy ones ; to the intent that the living may know that the Most High ruleth in the kingdom of men, and giveth it to whomsoever he will, and setteth up over it the basest of men."

There is in all this much of that incongruity which is characteristic of dreams ; yet the turn of the angel's words, whereby he indicated that the tree represented a man, and the moral purpose of the whole, as expressed in his concluding phrases, could not but impress the heart of Nebuchadnezzar ; and even before he had received the interpretation from Daniel, his conscience must have whispered that the tree was designed to represent himself. Just as, at a later day, the trembling of Belshazzar, when he saw the handwriting on the wall, was itself an interpretation, or, rather, the consequences of an interpretation, already made by himself of the mysterious characters, so the anxiety of Nebuchadnezzar here was the result of an application to himself of this singular vision. But his conscience gave him only a vague presentiment of its real meaning. So, wishing to discover the particular significance of each part of his dream, and regarding it as a revelation from Heaven, he sent for the Chaldeans to give him the explanation. One wonders that, after his former experience, he did not send for Daniel at once. But many years had elapsed since the date of the interpretation of the former dream, and the vivid impression made upon his mind at that time of the pre-eminence of Daniel's God had been effaced; so he resorted to the accredited source of light in his empire. But the Chaldeans were again at fault. They could not explain this dream, any more than they could reproduce the former.

At the last, however, Daniel, apparently without having been sent for, presented himself to the monarch, and after having heard the dream, he was so grieved at its meaning that he sat speechless for an hour, and only regained the power of utterance to say with the sincerest emotion, "My lord, the dream be to them that hate thee, and the interpretation thereof to thine enemies." He then, after recapitulating the various objects in the vision, gave the interpretation thus : " They shall drive thee from men, and thy dwelling shall be with the beasts of the field, and they shall make thee to eat grass as oxen, and they shall wet thee with the dew of heaven, and seven times shall pass over thee, till thou know that the Most High ruleth in the kingdom of men, and giveth it to whomsoever he will." Then, passing from the interpreter to the counsellor, the faithful prophet, valuing the welfare of the monarch more than his good opinion for the moment, and fearing degradation for him more than the loss of favor for himself, added these words, which are not more remarkable for the courtesy of their tone than for the sternness of their fidelity: "Wherefore, O king, let my counsel be acceptable unto thee, and break off thy sins by righteousness, and thine iniquities by showing mercy to the poor, if it may be a lengthening of thy tranquillity."

We do not know how this wise advice was received. Perhaps the monarch was too thankful to obtain an explanation of his dream to quarrel with the moral precepts of him who had interpreted it, and so, while inwardly chafing at the rebuke which was implied in Daniel's words, he may have smothered his indignation for the time, and allowed his servant to go as unreproved as he was unrewarded. But, however he felt at the moment, we know that no improvement characterized either his disposition or his conduct. For a full year things went on as before, and perhaps the king may have been congratulating himself that for once Daniel was wrong in his interpretation, or that the dream had no special significance. But though God's retribution may come slowly, it comes surely, and ere long all that Daniel had described was realized.

Looking forth from his palace over the city which he had done so much to beautify, extend, and fortify, he was in the very act of giving utterance to the pride with which his heart was swelling, when a great calamity came upon him. Scarcely had he said, "Is not this great Babylon, that I have built for the house of the kingdom by the might of my power, and for the honor of my majesty?" when a voice from heaven fell upon his ear repeating Daniel's prophecy. In the terror produced by this divine communication, his reason was dethroned, and he went forth a wretched maniac, leaving his kingdom to be cared for by his son, and living for seven times—that is, as some think, for seven years, after the manner of the beasts of the field.

Much has been written by commentators in all ages on this illness of Nebuchadnezzar; but it is generally agreed, from the use of these words in reference to his recovery, "Mine understanding returned unto me," that he became insane; and, from the description of the condition to which he was reduced, physiologists have concluded that he was afflicted with that species of madness in which "the sufferer, while retaining his consciousness in other respects, imagines himself to be changed into some animal, and acts up to a certain point in conformity with that persuasion. Those who imagined themselves changed into wolves howled like wolves, and (falsely, as there is reason to believe) accused themselves of bloodshed. Others imitated the cries of dogs."* The disease goes by the generic name of *zoanthropia*.

In the case before us, Nebuchadnezzar fancied himself an ox, and acted in conformity with that imagination, eating grass among the cattle, and remaining exposed in the fields to all weathers, until his hair became like the feathers of an eagle in length and matted consistency, and his nails like the claws of a bird. All this while, however, there must have been within him somewhat of a consciousness of his

---

* Pusey's "Lectures on Daniel the Prophet," pp. 428, 429. In the Bohn's Library edition of "Izaak Walton's Complete Angler," which I was consulting lately for quite another purpose, I find the following note on p. 166, by the American editor: "Among the many strange delusions which have afflicted men, that of supposing themselves transformed into brutes of various kinds, such as horses, dogs, wolves, or others, has been so frequent as to give names to several forms of mania, classed by Sauvages in his 'Nosology' under the general head of Zoanthropy. Raulin affirms that a whole cloister of nuns imagined themselves to be cats, mewing, etc., as such. A few years since there might have been seen, in the hospital of Bellevue, New York, a man who fancied himself to be a hog, and had attained singular skill in grunting as he rolled among the straw in his cell."

real identity, which must, one would think, have intensified to him the misery of his malady.

Dr. Pusey, in his " Lectures on Daniel," quotes the following sentences on this point from Dr. Browne, the Commissioner of the Board of Lunacy for Scotland, who speaks from an experience of thirty years : " My opinion is," says he, " that of all mental powers or conditions the idea of personal identity is but rarely enfeebled, and that it is never extinguished. The *ego* (self) and *non ego* (not self) may be confused. The *ego*, however, continues to preserve the personality. All the angels, devils, dukes, lords, kings, gods, many that I have had under my care, remained what they were before they became angels, dukes, etc., in a sense, and even nominally. I have seen a man declaring himself the Saviour, or St. Paul, yet sign his own name James Thomson, and attend worship as regularly as if the notion of Divinity had never entered into his head. I think it probable, therefore, because consistent with experience in similar forms of mental affection, that Nebuchadnezzar retained a perfect consciousness that he was Nebuchadnezzar during the whole course of his degradation."*

Some have supposed that the band of iron and brass which was to be put round the stump of the tree symbolizes the mode of restraint to which the maniac monarch was subjected, inasmuch as he was probably bound in chains, either to keep him from inflicting injury upon himself, or to prevent him from doing harm to others. But whether he was bound thus, or whether he was permitted to wander at his will among the cattle of the fields, we must equally see how much cause for gratitude we in these days have in the fact that, owing to the advance of medical science, insanity is recognized as a disease, just as much and as really as a

---

* Pusey's " Lectures on Daniel the Prophet," pp. 430, 435.

fever is, and that those who are afflicted with it are in the main treated with gentleness, and in such a way as shall best conduce to the restoration of health to the brain. It is always a terrible affliction; it is indeed, in my view, the most painful form of disease to which our complex humanity is liable; and when one sees a man endowed with such strength of mind as Nebuchadnezzar possessed, yet reduced to such a pitiable condition, one is led to thank God as he never did before for the continuance of his reason, and to pray that he may be preserved from similar distress. For if Dr. Browne's idea that the king kept all through the consciousness that he was Nebuchadnezzar be correct, his agony must at times have been most acute; and if this were the time or place, or if it were needed to bring out more forcibly the point on which I am now insisting, we might quote from the recorded experience of others in similar circumstances, how bitterly they felt the humiliation of their condition. What an anguish it was now and then to Robert Hall, with that noble intellect of his, to awake to the fact, as he sometimes did after a paroxysm of madness, that he had become so irrational! And similar shocks of agony must have gone through the heart of Nebuchadnezzar during his time of affliction.

But, after the seven times had gone, the king lifted up his eyes unto heaven, and his understanding came to him again, but came in a form more clear than before, for now he perceived that his greatness was not all his own. He discovered that he had nothing which he had not received, and he was disposed to give to the Most High God the glory of all that he was, and all that he had done. With this recognition of the King eternal, immortal, and invisible, the only wise God, his reason came to him, and the glory of his kingdom and the honor and the brightness of his court were restored, and his " counsellors and his lords sought again to him, and he was established in his kingdom."

It has been thought a strange thing that no record of this mental eclipse of Nebuchadnezzar should be found in the ancient historians of his times. But the silence of these authors may, perhaps, be thus accounted for. Berosus, being himself a native of Babylon, and having what one may call a pardonable pride in the greatness of Nebuchadnezzar, the most illustrious monarch of the empire, may have been tempted to suppress this incident, lest it should seem to mar the splendor of his renown ; and as for Herodotus, he did not visit Babylon till one hundred years after the death of Nebuchadnezzar, and it may well be doubted if he ever heard anything about that monarch's madness. But recently a portion of the great Standard Inscription, among the Cuneiform memorials of the empire, has been brought to light by Rawlinson, which, to say the least of it, seems to contain an allusion to the singular hiatus in his reign which his lunacy produced. I quote the passage as it is given in Smith's " Dictionary of the Bible :"

" After describing the construction of the most important of his great works, he appears to say, ' For four years the seat of my kingdom did not rejoice my heart. In all my dominions I did not build a high place of power ; the precious treasures of my kingdom I did not lay up. In Babylon, buildings for myself and for the honor of my kingdom I did not lay out. In the worship of Merodach, my lord, the joy of my heart, in Babylon, the seat of his sovereignty, and the seat of my empire, I did not sing his praises ; I did not furnish his altars with victims, nor did I clear out the canals.' Other negative clauses follow. It is plain that we have here narrated a suspension, apparently for four years, of all those works and occupations on which the king especially prided himself—his temples, palaces, worship, offerings, and works of irrigation; and though the cause of the suspension is not stated, we can scarcely imagine anything that would account for it but some such extraordinary malady as that recorded in Daniel."* To say the least of it, we have here a very singular coincidence, and we may fairly enough adduce this strange passage from the Standard Inscription as counterbalancing the silence of the ancient historians upon the subject.

But now the question presents itself, What did Nebuchadnezzar design by the publication of the decree in which these facts are here preserved? Did he mean to represent himself as having become an adherent of the Jewish faith? Did he put this forth as an account of what we, in modern phrase, would call his "conversion?" Was he, after the publication of this decree, or, rather, after the occurrences on which it is founded, a truly regenerate man, a real and devout believer in Jehovah as the only living and true God?

These questions are much more easily asked than answered. On the one hand, there is much in the document which looks as if the king had become a believer in the unity and supremacy of Jehovah, as when he speaks of him as the Most High, of his dominion as everlasting, and of his authority as absolute. On the other hand, there are detached expressions which seem to indicate that he was still a worshipper of the inferior deities of polytheism. Thus, he names Daniel "Belteshazzar," adding the clause, "according to the name of my God," and says of him, "in whom is the spirit of the holy gods." It would appear, therefore, that, while acknowledging the supremacy of Jehovah as the Most High, he still clung to the worship and service of inferior divinities. Hence, though there was what might be

---

* Smith's "Dictionary," vol. ii., p. 483.

called a conversion in him, it was still an imperfect conversion. He did not allow his belief in a supreme God to interfere with the acknowledgment of inferior gods. Just as Cyrus, in his edict, owned the supremacy of the God of Israel, and Artaxerxes spoke of him as the God of heaven, while neither of them, so far as we know, abjured the polytheism in which they had both been educated; so it is not improbable that Nebuchadnezzar was brought, by the influence of his affliction, to recognize the supreme power of Jehovah while yet he retained his worship of other deities. This reading of his character, too, is most in harmony with his intense devotion to the idol Bel-Merodach, which, as we saw in our former lecture, comes out in the great Cuneiform inscription to which I have so frequently alluded.

But it must also be admitted that there is much in the document before us to incline us to believe that he became a really renewed man. Hence we find the commentator Scott saying, with his usual caution, "The beginning and conclusion of this chapter lead us at least to hope with prevailing confidence that he was at last made a monument of the power of divine grace and the exceeding riches of divine mercy;" and Matthew Henry thus similarly concludes his interesting comment on this chapter: "Whether he continued in the same good mind that here he seems to have been in we are not told, nor doth anything appear to the contrary but that he did; and if so great a blasphemer and persecutor did find mercy, he was not the last. And if our charity reach so far as to hope that he did, we must admire free grace, by which he lost his wits for a while that he might save his soul forever."

I undertake not to decide where so much uncertainty is felt by every candid reader. Long since the king has gone to his account, and we may be sure that the Judge of all the earth will do right regarding him. Hence, without dwelling further on a point which we cannot settle, let us see what lessons we may glean for ourselves from this deeply interesting record.

And, first, we have here a solemn and instructive warning against pride and vainglory. With all his ability, Nebuchadnezzar had nothing which he had not received from God. His intellectual greatness, his military success, his architectural triumphs, all were gifts to him from Jehovah; and if he had humbly and cheerfully acknowledged this, and given God the glory, he would have been yet greater in his piety and humility than he was in all his other excellencies put together. What a difference between him and Daniel in this respect! When the young captive had reproduced and interpreted the vision of the composite image, and was afterward complimented for it by the king, he was careful first to say, "As for me, this secret is not revealed to me for any wisdom that I have more than any living, but for their sakes that shall make known the interpretation to the king, and that thou mightest know the thoughts of thy heart."

How much more attractive is the example of the prophet than that of the monarch! In which of them, brethren, do we see ourselves? For let us not imagine that such pride as Nebuchadnezzar evinced is manifested by kings and earthly grandees alone. It may be as really existent in the heart of some one here to-night as it was in that of the Babylonian emperor. Whoever plumes himself upon what he has done in the world, as if he were the author of it all, and not simply the instrument in the hand of God, is as really and truly proud and haughty as was Nebuchadnezzar here. The merchant, who speaks of his business as the sole result of his ability, and calls himself, with supreme satisfaction, "the architect of his own fortunes;" the author, who thinks of his book as the creation of his own genius; the statesman, who looks upon his position as entirely self-made; the artisan, who prides himself upon his foremanship; and the millionnaire, who, looking upon his glittering heaps, congratulates himself as the sole author of his gains—all alike are guilty of Nebuchadnezzar's sin; for they have shut God out of their hearts, and they have not given him the acknowledgment and the honor to which he is entitled.

Let us seek, therefore, each to be clothed with humility, and, wherever we are and whatever we have, let us acknowledge God. "Every good gift and every perfect gift cometh down" from him, and to him we should give all the honor. In heaven they cast their crowns before the throne, implying that only by the favor of him who sits thereon have they crowns at all; and it should be the same on earth. The prizes we win in the race of life should be won by us that we may put them into Jehovah's hand. This would sanctify the race itself, and this would take away the danger of success. The full cup is difficult to carry; let us, therefore, pour it out before the Lord. The lofty height makes one dizzy as he looks down and begins to think that he has by his own power toiled up the steep; but when, looking up, he sees how far he is still beneath God, and cries for the continuance of his holding and helping hand, he is steadied again, and renews his ascent. Let us, therefore, guard against pride, and learn of him who said, "I am lowly."

We have here a sad illustration of the proverb that "pride goeth before a fall." Sooner or later, the spirit which I have been now exposing will bring punishment upon him who cherishes it, and the punishment will be of such a nature as to make the sinner see and know the heinousness of his sin.

You cannot read this chapter without remembering that other record in the Acts of the Apostles: "And upon a set day Herod, arrayed in royal apparel, sat upon his throne, and made an oration unto them. And the people gave a shout, saying, It is the voice of a god, and not of a man.

And immediately the angel of the Lord smote him, *because he gave not God the glory:* and he was eaten of worms, and gave up the ghost."* Which of us, also, has not recalled to his memory the parable of the rich fool, to whom, while he was in the act of congratulating himself on his prosperity, and planning barns and buildings new, it was said, "Thou fool, this night thy soul shall be required of thee?"† Ah, it is a fearful thing to make a god of one's self. Hath not Jehovah's prophet said, "The idols he shall utterly abolish;" and if that idol in our case be self, think you self will not by him be degraded and destroyed? But not without warning do his strokes fall. Many years were given to the antediluvians before the flood came and submerged them, and twelve months of grace were given to Nebuchadnezzar here before the blow was struck which made his reason reel. So yet Jehovah warns those who are in the path of danger; and who can tell but the discourse of this evening may be by him designed to be to some proud and haughty sinner here, what this dream and its interpretation were to Nebuchadnezzar? Oh! let the proud take warning, and "humble themselves under the mighty hand of God, that he may exalt them in due time."

In the third place, we have here a beautiful illustration of fidelity in the proclamation of God's truth. It cost Daniel a great deal to give this interpretation of the dream to the monarch. The king had been very kind to him, and he would rather have done a great many other things than have unfolded to him all that was declared by the vision. But there was no help for it! Necessity was laid upon him, and faithfulness alike to Jehovah and to Nebuchadnezzar required that he should speak the whole truth. Hence he gave the interpretation with the utmost exactness; and then,

---

* Acts xii., 21–23.   † Luke xii., 15–21.

in the most courteous manner, he advised the king to re-
·pentance. Now, only they who have had to say unwelcome
truths to those who are above them in station, or to whom in
worldly matters they have been much beholden, can estimate
the difficulty and delicacy of the position which the prophet
occupied. Many in his place would have evaded the duty
altogether, and held their peace. Many others, perhaps,
under the plea of being faithful, would have become imper-
·tinent, and used language both uncourtly and unwarranted.
But what could be finer than Daniel's bearing all through?
With manifest sorrow the interpretation is given, and after
that is finished there is this brief and beautiful application
made: "Wherefore, O king, let my counsel be acceptable
unto thee, and break off thy sins by righteousness, and thine
iniquities by showing mercy to the poor, if it may be a
lengthening of thy tranquillity." What an example have we
here to every messenger of God! Equally removed from
time-serving timidity and impertinent rudeness, he sets the
truth in loving faithfulness before his master, and behold
his reward! Perhaps the king was annoyed in the first instance, but he lived to value the advice, and here five years
—yea, perhaps eight years—after it had been given, it is reproduced by the monarch himself, and inserted in his decree to show how much he came at length to value the
friendship of his servant. May God help every preacher of
his truth to be as faithful and as courteous as was Daniel
here!

In the fourth place, we have surely a loud call addressed
to us in this chapter to thank God for the continuance of
our reason. How seldom we think of this! Yet how important it is, after all! What a blessing it is to have a
sound mind in a sound body! Let us praise God for its
possession, and let us use means for its preservation. I do
not think that we in this age are nearly so careful in this

respect as we ought to be. We are living at high-pressure.
We are going, intellectually, at express speed; and so, not
unfrequently, our finest minds are ruined, and our most useful men rendered mentally incapable of serving either their
country or their age. Others there are who wilfully court
insanity, and by excesses of sensuality and intemperance
sow the seeds of disease in the brain whereby, at length,
their intellects are clouded and their end is darkened. Let
us avoid all this. Let us show our gratitude to God for our
reason, not only by the ascription of praise to him for its
possession, but also by using it in his service, and by doing
our best to preserve it for his glory.

In the fifth place, we are here reminded that the Most
High ruleth in the kingdoms of men. God is the King of
kings; and however men may plan and scheme, however
they may make war and peace, whatsoever laws they may
proclaim or treaties they may sign, "he doeth according to
his will among the armies of heaven and among the inhabitants of the earth." How this can be, while yet men are
free agents, uncoerced in any way, and following only the
inclinations of their own hearts, we cannot tell; but so it is.
"There are many devices in a man's heart; nevertheless
the counsel of the Lord, that shall stand." Herod schemes,
and Pilate trims, according to the nature of each; yet the
result is the doing of what God's "hand and counsel determined before to be done." And the same is true yet.
Amidst wars and revolutions, amidst the schemings of emperors and chancellors, seeking only their own aggrandize-
ment, God is ruling still; and he will bring out, clear and
definite at last, before men's eyes, the much-forgotten truth
that the allegiance of their hearts is due to him. This is
our comfort amidst the movements of our times. No doubt,
as men pursue their schemes and rage in their ambition, he
may seem asleep, as Jesus was in the little boat upon the

lake; but by-and-by he will awake and cry, "Peace, be still;" and in the calm thereby produced the Church will go forward on its glorious mission, and gather in the saved into its bosom. There is one who can say, and who will say, at the proper time, to Czar and Sultan alike, "Hitherto shall ye come, but no further: and here shall your proud waves be stayed." There is one of whom it is written, "He maketh the wrath of man to praise him, and restraineth the remainder thereof." If this be true, then how safe the counsel of the Psalmist, himself a king, "Be wise now therefore, O ye kings: be instructed, ye judges of the earth. Serve the Lord with fear, and rejoice with trembling. Kiss the Son, lest he be angry, and ye perish from the way, when his wrath is kindled but a little. Blessed are all they that put their trust in him." And for ourselves, why should we wait till a judgment teaches us this truth as it was taught to Nebuchadnezzar? Let us to-night submit ourselves to God through Jesus Christ, and yield to him the throne of our hearts and the homage of our lives.

VI.

BELSHAZZAR'S FEAST.

DANIEL V., 1–31.

A S in certain important particulars, the narrative contained in this chapter seems to be at variance with the
records of ancient historians, it will be necessary, before proceeding to make any practical use of its incidents, that we
vindicate the accuracy of the inspired writer. That the issue
may be clearly set before you, let me give a brief summary
of the events of the period, collected and condensed from
the articles in the Dictionaries of Smith, Fairbairn, and Kitto.

Nebuchadnezzar at his death (561 B.C.) was succeeded by
his son Evil-Merodach, who, after having held the crown for
two years, was murdered by his brother-in-law, Neriglissar,
who reigned for four years. After him came his son Labo-
rosoarchod, a mere lad, who, nine months after his succession to the throne, fell a victim to a conspiracy, and was succeeded by Nabonnedus, who mounted the throne very shortly before the war broke out between Cyrus and Crœsus.
He chose to ally himself with Crœsus, and this provoked
the hostility of Cyrus, who determined to attack him and
destroy his power.

Now, according to the ancient historian Berosus, this Nabonnedus was the last king of Babylon. And so far from being slain in Babylon, we are told that he went out to meet
Cyrus in battle, and being defeated by him, took refuge in
the stronghold of Borsippa, but soon after surrendered to
the conqueror, and being kindly treated by him, was allowed
to retire to Carmania, where he died.

It thus appears that there were more monarchs than one in the line of succession between Nebuchadnezzar and Nabonnedus, and that Daniel, in referring to Belshazzar, cannot be speaking of the king whom Berosus has described. Of course, the antagonists of Scripture have made a great deal of this, and in former days they were accustomed to refer to it as a hopeless discrepancy. But, in a marvellous manner, God has in these later times triumphantly vindicated the accuracy of his servant. It was always evident that Daniel had not spoken of Belshazzar as the immediate successor of Nebuchadnezzar, and no anxiety was felt by the defenders of Scripture in regard to that; but now, from the resurrection of long-buried monuments, the missing link has been discovered by which we can easily establish the accuracy both of the sacred writer and the profane historians.

In the year 1854, Sir Henry Rawlinson deciphered the inscriptions on some cylinders found in the ruins of Um-Gheir (the ancient Ur of the Chaldees) containing memorials of the works executed by Nabonnedus. From these it appears that the eldest son of Nabonnedus was called Bel-shar-ezar, and admitted by his father to a share in the government. In a communication to the *Athenæum* (No. 1377), Sir Henry Rawlinson says: "We can now understand how Belshazzar, as joint king with his father, may have been governor of Babylon when the city was attacked by the combined forces of the Medes and Persians, and may have perished in the assault which followed, while Nabonnedus, leading a force to the relief of the place, was defeated, and obliged to take refuge in Borsippa, capitulating after a short resistance, and being subsequently assigned an honorable retirement in Carmania."[*]

But if this be so, you are ready to ask how it comes that

---

[*] Smith's "Dictionary," article BELSHAZZAR.

Belshazzar is here called the son of Nebuchadnezzar. To which I answer that in the East the term "son" is used with great latitude of meaning, and may refer to a nephew or a grandson, as well as a son proper. Now, Rawlinson supposes that Nabonnedus married the daughter of Nebuchadnezzar, an alliance which would account for his conspiring to get the throne, and thus Belshazzar would be the grandson of that monarch.

I have been thus particular in entering upon these details that you may see how wonderfully God in his providence, by the disentombing of these old cylinders, is putting Rationalism and Infidelity to silence, and that your faith may be strengthened in reference to those remaining historical difficulties in the Sacred Scriptures for which, as yet, no satisfactory solution has been given.

The only other point that needs to be adverted to is the naming of Darius the Mede in the last verse of the chapter. All ancient historians agree that Babylon was taken by Cyrus in person. How comes it, then, that here in the closing verse it is said "Darius the Mede took the kingdom, being about threescore years old?" To this I reply that it is not said that Darius was the general under whom the city of Babylon was taken, but simply that he took the kingdom, a mode of speech which is perfectly consistent with the fact that Cyrus took the city, if we suppose that after he had taken it, he left Darius there as his delegate and representative, to exercise the regal authority while he went on with his military campaign.

But now having, as I trust, satisfactorily disposed of the historical questions arising out of this chapter, let me proceed to the consideration of its contents, having a special regard to their bearing upon ourselves.

The character of Belshazzar appears to have been of the most contemptible description. He was addicted to the lowest vices of self-indulgence, and felt no restraint whatever in the gratification of his desires. With all this there was combined an arrogance of the haughtiest kind, which would brook no interference with his designs, and would submit to no expostulation in the interests of morality. The severe lesson read by Jehovah to his grandfather in that mysterious malady with which he had been so long afflicted was entirely lost on him; and he went on to greater and greater excesses, as if to show that he had no regard whatever either for God or man. At length, however, the cup of his iniquities became full. In an hour when he was not aware of it, the Son of man came; and he who "being often reproved had hardened his neck, was suddenly cut off, and that without remedy."

Briefly let us enumerate the horrors of that dreadful night, in the hope that his case may prove a beacon for us, and keep us from the rock on which he wrecked his kingdom and lost his soul.

Notice, first, the intemperance by which this banquet was characterized. With the whole number of his lords, and surrounded by his wives and concubines, he held high festival; and with particular emphasis, as if to mark his own excess, it is said that "he drank wine before the thousand." He had not heard, perhaps—or if he had, he only disregarded—the good Hebrew proverb, "It is not for kings, O Lemuel, it is not for kings to drink wine; nor for princes strong drink: lest they drink, and forget the law, and pervert the judgment of any of the afflicted."* He cared for nothing then but the revelry of the hour. He kept the wine-cup circling round; and we may be sure that the example which he set would be followed by the members of his court, if, indeed, they did not outrun him in the unholy race. For

---

* Proverbs xxxi., 4, 5.

when the giver of a feast is himself a man of temperate habits, there is commonly some slight restraint upon his companions ; but when he is a leader in dissipation, "it shall go hard but they will better his instruction." This last, we doubt not, was the case here ; and so, as the maddening poison did its wonted work, the tongues of that multitude would be loosed, and the noise and confusion would be as great as that from which their city first received its name.

Alas! we know only too well the concomitants of an excess like this ; for such a scene is not confined to a heathen country, with a godless Belshazzar for its king. The same intemperance exists even now among ourselves. We have many national sins, and I am not now prepared to say which of them is the greatest ; but it is indisputable that among them all drunkenness holds a prominent position. I will not stop to compare our land with other countries in regard to it. I ask you only to walk with open eyes through the streets that line these two rivers. Who knows not the drunkard's staggering gait, and tattered garments, and stupid, unmeaning countenance, compared with which that of the gorilla is intelligence itself ? and who has not seen him all too often reeling past or rolling in the gutter ? Go where we may, too, we see those crime-manufacturing saloons, alluring men to their destruction. Nay, as if their existence were a blessing, they are multiplied on every hand, so that in New York city alone we have no fewer than eight thousand of them—enough to make a street of more than ten miles in length, and consuming somewhere about fifty millions of dollars annually. In these circumstances, what can be expected but the increase of that vice which is eating like a canker into the heart of our social life, and gnawing at the root of our national pre-eminence ?

Some one has beautifully compared our social system to a pyramid, with its broad base resting on the mass of the

people, and its sides rising up, through legislators and governors, until they reach the apex in the chief magistrate of
the republic, and has said that this is the most stable form
of government. And so, doubtless, it is, if you have sound
materials out of which to build your pyramid. But if the
mass of the people who form its base—and that is the most
important part of it—should become corrupt, what can keep
the fabric from falling to the dust? A corrupt government
and a foolish legislature may do much to mar the beauty of
a country and arrest its progress; but, provided the great
heart of the people be sound, the nation will rise and recover its old renown. If, however, the millions of the population should degenerate, if their manhood should be eaten
out of them by intemperance, neither Government nor Con-
gress will be able to prevent the national decay that must
ensue. As patriots, therefore, not to speak at present of the
higher duty of our Christian profession, it becomes us to do
our utmost to arrest this mighty evil. I prescribe not here
how you are to deal with it. I only ask each of you consci-
entiously, and as in the sight of the Redeemer's cross, to
face the question, "What ought I to do in this regard?"
and, if I may judge from my own experience, I feel convinced that every man who sets himself to grapple with that
question fairly will determine that, in present circumstances,
he, at least, will have nothing whatever to do with the ac-
cursed thing.

And oh! if there be any one here to-night who knows that
he is personally addicted to this vice, let me implore him
never again to taste strong drink. "Look not thou on the
wine when it is red, when it giveth its color in the cup, when
it moveth itself aright. At the last, it biteth like a serpent,
and stingeth like an adder." "*At the last!*" Would you
know what that means? Then come with me, and see the
saddest sight, I think, I ever witnessed. The warden was

leading me through one of the corridors of the workhouse
on Blackwell's Island, when, going to the door of a cell, he
pushed back the sliding board from the grating and bade
me look in.　The room was lighted by a small window near
the ceiling.　All around, to the height of perhaps eight feet
or more, it was lined with padding covered with leather, and
on the floor, spread over its entire breadth, there was a mattress having a similar appearance to the padding on the
sides.　On the mattress there lay a man, probably not more
than five-and-twenty years of age, bareheaded, barefooted,
stripped of coat and vest, and having his arms tightly bound
behind him with strong cords.　He had dropped asleep for
a moment or two, and was breathing heavily.　"There!"
said the warden, as he turned away, "that is the end of his
debauch.　He is suffering from delirium tremens, and we
have put him in there to keep him from injuring himself."
Ah! thought I, he is somebody's son ; and my heart bled
as I looked upon his degradation.　This is what it comes
to "at the last!"　Yet that, after all, is not the last ; for the
book before me says, "No drunkard shall inherit the kingdom of heaven."　O thou! whosoever thou art, who art the
victim of this appetite, wilt thou lay these things to heart?
I know thou feelest thy slavery and hatest thy chains ; but
if thou wouldst be free, thyself, by God's help, "must strike
the blow."　Rise, then, in the might of thy manhood, and,
by the supplicated help of God's Holy Spirit, snap asun-
der the bands wherewith thine enemy has bound thee.　Remember Belshazzar, and fling away thy cup ere yet thou art
overtaken by Belshazzar's doom !

But notice, secondly, the profanity by which this banquet
was characterized.　The king called for the sacred vessels
which his grandfather had brought from the Temple of Jerusalem, and he desecrated them by employing them in his
idolatrous orgies.　Observe, it is said that he did this "while

he tasted the wine," and as a consequence, doubtless, of the excitement produced in him by the drinking of it. It is always thus.

There is an old fable which tells of a man who had the choice which of three sins he would commit—drunkenness, adultery, or murder. He chose drunkenness as being apparently the least; but when he was intoxicated, so the story runs, he committed both the others, and thus ended by being guilty of all the three. There is deep meaning in the fable; for who shall reckon up for us the number of crimes committed under the influence of strong drink? crimes from the very thought of which the individuals who perpetrated them would in their sober senses have shrunk back appalled.

. In the case before us, it could not but be that the impression of Jehovah's greatness which had been produced upon Nebuchadnezzar, and through him upon the nation at large, had remained at least in some measure, and if soberness had ruled the hour, instead of excess, we may well believe that Belshazzar and his lords would have recoiled from doing such indignity to the God of the Hebrews. Idolaters though they were, the very regard which they paid to their own divinities, not to speak of the remembrance of the fiery furnace out of which Jehovah had delivered his servants, might have taught them reverence for the vessels of the Temple; but no: "They drank and praised" (that is, "toasted," for in this heathen practice our modern custom, "more honored in the breach than in the observance," had its origin) "the gods of gold and of silver, of brass, of iron, of wood and of stone."

Now, it is not possible for us to commit this sin of theirs precisely in the same form as that in which they committed it, since there are not among us, as in the Jewish Temple there were, vessels specially and peculiarly consecrated to

God. But in other forms, alas! profanity too is rampant in the midst of us. Who among us has not often had his ears pained and his heart sickened by the unhallowed use of the names of God by those who have no reverence for him in their hearts? In the workshop and in the store, as well as on the street and in the haunts of riot and iniquity, one may hear the dear name of Jesus garnishing an oath, and horrid imprecations at which our hair does stand on end are become common even among the children on our streets.

Oh that men would remember that holy law which says that "the Lord will not hold him guiltless that taketh his name in vain!" Oh that they would think of the sinfulness of their profanity! They talk of it as a habit; they acknowledge it to be ungenteel; and they will ask pardon of those before whom they have spoken the horrid words, especially if there should chance to be a minister among them; but they think not of the guilt of profane swearing before God! Truly, as one has said, the swearer serves the devil for nothing. "Men do not despise a thief if he steal to satisfy his soul when he is hungry;" and there may be some extenuation for other forms of evil; but what does the swearer gain by his profanity? It is a wanton insult to the majesty and love of God. Be it yours, my hearers, not only to abstain from this iniquity yourselves, but also to check and reprove it wherever it is committed by others. Keep your lips from this evil, and to this end let your hearts be filled with love to Jesus and reverence for God, so that the first petition of the Master's prayer may be daily answered in your life as well as offered by your lips, "Hallowed be thy name."

Notice, thirdly, that this night was one of supernatural visitation. Fast flew the hours, and boisterous was the mirth; merrily the laugh went round, and the cup was passed from hand to hand. Who cares though the Mede

be at the gates and all around the walls? Are there not
two years' provisions within the city? and will not its fer-
tile terraces yield more, if so much be required? Let fear
be laughed to scorn, or drowned in the flowing bowl! On
with the revelry; let it know no pause until the morning
light! But, ah! what means that sudden lull in the noisy
revel—that break in the madness of the mirth? Each eye
runs along the hall, and in a moment all are fixed upon the
king. Wildly he looks, with fixed and steady glare, upon
the wall before him, his eyeballs almost starting from their
sockets. Big bead-like drops of perspiration stand upon
his forehead; a deathly paleness sits upon his countenance;
the uplifted goblet falls from his palsied hands, and his
knees smite one upon another. "The king! the king!
what aileth him?" is now the cry. But he gives no verbal
answer. He simply points, with a new shudder of agony,
to the spot on which his gaze is fixed; and, as they look
there with him, they, too, see the fingers of a hand, tracing,
all solemnly and slowly, mysterious characters upon the wall.

Sobered on the instant by this dread appearance, they
summon forthwith to the royal presence the astrologers,
the Chaldeans, and soothsayers, if haply they may be able
to decipher the strange writing. But they are completely
baffled; and the king, too surely foreboding its true meaning, sinks into remorse and dark despair. Where now the
daring spirit of the sacrilegious idolaters? Where now the
mirth the wine provoked? Silence, as of the grave, reigns
in the hall, so late the scene of jollity and noise. In his
perplexity the queen-mother comes in, and reminds him of
a servant whom he had long neglected, and whose warnings
he had oft despised. She tells him of Daniel, and his great
service on a similar occasion, in the reign of Nebuchadnezzar; and, at her suggestion, the Hebrew prophet is brought
in before him. Sternly the man of God (repudiating his

proffered gifts) reminds him of the noble opportunity he possessed of serving God; of the warning that had been given to his grandfather; of his own pride, idolatry, sacrilege; and, most of all, of this—the one fatal omission of his whole life—that "he had not glorified the God in whose hands his breath was, and whose were all his ways;" and then, without a word of hope, or exhortation, or even of pity, he reads out his doom: "God hath numbered thy kingdom, and finished it." "Thou art weighed in the balances, and art found wanting." "Thy kingdom is divided, and given to the Medes and Persians."

No ray of hope brightens the gloom of that awful sentence; it is dark, dark, eternally dark. And why so? Brethren, let us hear the answer, and be warned by this example. It was because Belshazzar had sinned away his "day of grace." Long before, when Daniel had been the messenger of God to Nebuchadnezzar, he had counselled him to break off his sins by righteousness, and his iniquities by showing mercy to the poor, if it might be a lengthening of his tranquillity. But there is no such exhortation now, for Belshazzar had systematically rejected all counsel from the Lord; and now, in the hour of his distress, the Lord abandons him, saying, "Because I called, and thou didst refuse, because I stretched out my hand, and thou didst not regard, I will laugh at thy calamity, and mock when thy fear cometh." It is now too late. The door of grace is shut. And as Belshazzar comes thundering at it, crying, "Open unto me!" the answer is returned, "Depart from me; I know thee not, thou worker of iniquity."

O sinner! will you take warning from a case like this? Beware lest, in your continued resistance to God's authority, you overstep that mysterious boundary that separates his forbearance and his wrath, and he be provoked to give you over to your own heart's lusts. I dare not say of any of you that you *have* crossed that limit; least of all can I say it of those who most fear lest they have, for the very existence of that fear is proof that they have not. But I desire to put you on your guard against it; I have to warn you that there is a danger of your doing it, and to urge you to come now, while you may, and avail yourself of God's mercy in Christ Jesus.

"*Too late!*"—there are no more melancholy words in the language than these. *Too late!*—I have heard them uttered by a brother, as, hurried home to see a dying father, he arrived only to be told that he had breathed his last; and not soon shall I forget the agony they then expressed. *Too late!* —I have known them uttered by a skilful surgeon, when he was summoned to the bedside of a dying man, and I have marked the sadness to which they then gave birth. *Too late!* —I have heard of them uttered by an anxious crowd, as they stood gazing on a burning dwelling, and sadly saw the failure of those who sought to save the inmates from destruction. *Too late!*—I have known them uttered by the noble crew of the life-boat, when, as they put out to the sinking ship, they beheld her go down before their eyes, and "the freighted souls within her." But, oh! none of these circumstances are half so heart-rending as those in which the sinner who has despised his day must find himself when the terrible discovery is made that he is *too late* to enter heaven. Very powerfully has the English laureate set this lesson to the music of his verse, in one of those lyrics which are the gems of the "Idyls of the King:"

> "Late, late, so late! and dark the night and chill!
> Late, late, so late! but we can enter still.
> Too late, too late! ye cannot enter now.

> "No light had we: for that we do repent;
> And learning this, the bridegroom will relent.
> Too late, too late! ye cannot enter now.

"No light: so late! and dark and chill the night!
Oh, let us in, that we may find the light!
Too late, too late! ye cannot enter now.

"Have we not heard the bridegroom is so sweet?
Oh, let us in, though late, to kiss his feet!
No, no, too late! ye cannot enter now."

Oh, may God grant that this sad exclusion may not be the doom of any one of us!

Notice, finally, that this was a night of terrible retribution. Not long was the execution of the sentence deferred after it had been pronounced; for ere the morning dawned Belshazzar was among the dead, and Babylon was in the Medo-Persians' hands. The manner in which this was brought about is described alike by Herodotus and Xenophon, and is in exact correspondence with the prophecy in the fiftieth and fifty-first chapters of Jeremiah. Cyrus, who had command of the besieging army, had lain for a long time before the city, and had almost despaired of taking it, when, hearing of an artificial lake which a former queen had made, he formed the plan of turning the waters of the Euphrates into that old and now dry lake-bed, and so rendering the river fordable at the city. To understand it further, it must be remembered that the Euphrates divided the city into two equal parts; that on each bank of the river twenty-five streets ran at right angles to the river, and parallel to each other; while the whole was surrounded by a wall sixty miles in circumference. The wall was carried over the river at each end of the town by a bridge; and at the end of each street, on the river-side, there were large, massive gates, which were locked nightly. When the waters had been diverted from their channel, the troops stationed at either end waded through below the bridges, the stream taking them only up to the loins. But even although they had reached so far, they would still have been stopped by the gates, had it not been for the fact that, owing to the prevalence of dissipation and carousal, consequent, as Herodotus says, on its being a festival night, the gates were carelessly, and contrary to usual custom, left open. Thus, at each end an entrance was effected, and the words of Jeremiah were fulfilled : "One post shall run to meet another, to show that the city is taken at the end," or, as the word might be better rendered, "at the two ends — endwise." Having thus got into the city, the Median troops advanced on toward the palace, and to their swords Belshazzar fell a victim.

My brethren, when God threatens, he means what he says, and he will bring it to pass. He is never at a loss for instruments ; and he will do whatsoever he hath spoken. Men seem to act as if he would prove faithful only to his promises ; but that is a miserable delusion. God is faithful who has threatened ; and, O sinner ! he has threatened thee with wrath if thou repent not. Think not, therefore, that thou shalt escape his just judgment, unless now thou betake thyself to him in Christ. His threatenings are no mere utterances of passion, soon to pass away, as the storm passes from the face of ocean ; they have their root in his very nature, and he must cease to be what he is if he fail to carry them out. The very same principle of his nature that leads him to keep his promises disposes him also to perform his threatenings ; and wherever we have the one manifestation of it, we have the other also, like the shadow following the sunlight.

You think of Noah in the Ark, and as you hear his evening psalm ascend from out his place of safety, you say, "God is faithful who has promised ;" but as you look around upon the wide waste of waters that has covered the earth, and hear the gurgling cry of some strong swimmer as he sinks beneath the wave, you are compelled to add, "God is faithful who has threatened." You think of Lot, angel-guided out of Sodom, and though he were saved yet so as by fire, you say, "God is faithful who has promised;" but when, with Abraham, in the early morning, you look over the plain, and see the smoke of the country ascending like the smoke of a furnace, you are made to add, "God is faithful who has threatened." You behold the tribes of Israel standing on the Red Sea shore, and as you hear their glorious anthem ring out above the noise of the waves, you say, "God is faithful who has promised;" but as you look behind, and mark how the refluent billows have submerged the haughty host of Pharaoh, you are constrained to say again, "God is faithful who has threatened." You think of the last grand assize, and as you behold the righteous going into life eternal you can hear them sing, "God is faithful who has promised;" while from out the mingled sobs and groans of the wicked, as they are driven to their own place, there rise these solemn words, "God is faithful who has threatened."

Let, then, the promises of the Lord win you to repentance, and the threatenings of Jehovah warn you from impenitency. Yea, even now, turn and look to Jesus, so that, when weighed in the balances at last, you may not be found wanting, but may stand in him. "Turn, and live ye;" there is the promise. "If he turn not, he will whet his sword. He hath bent his bow, and made it ready;" there is the threatening. Make thy choice between them.

VII.

DANIEL IN THE DEN.

THE question who this Darius the Mede was has greatly perplexed the commentators on the Book of Daniel; but it would serve no good purpose to enter here upon
its minute investigation. Let it suffice to say that the answer which seems to me to be beset with fewest difficulties
is that which regards him as Cyaxeres the Second, the uncle
and father-in-law of Cyrus. This view at once harmonizes
with the statement of Xenophon, that he was the son of Astyages, and ascended the throne after him, and with that of
Josephus, who affirms that "he was the son of Astyages, but
had another name among the Greeks;" while, at the same
time, it accounts for the fact mentioned in the concluding
verse of the preceding chapter, that at the taking of Babylon he was about sixty two years of age. It is right to say,
however, that this is only one of three different opinions
which have been advocated, and that probably we must wait
for the correct solution of the difficulty until some Babylonian inscription furnishes the data on which it can be made.

For the better management of the empire, Darius divided
it into one hundred and twenty provinces, over each of
which he appointed a responsible officer. Over these, again,
he set three presidents or satraps, and, as the chief of these,
he named Daniel, "because he had an excellent spirit in
him." These presidents corresponded somewhat to modern secretaries of state, while Daniel, as the head over them

all, was in a position similar to that of the prime minister
of a European kingdom, or like the grand-vizier of an Eastern empire.

His elevation to this dignity need not be in the least degree surprising unto us; for altogether irrespective of the
special providence which watched over him, and which was
as clearly conspicuous in his life as in that of Joseph, we
may account for his exaltation to this new dignity on pure-
ly natural principles. When Darius entered Babylon, he
would find every one talking of the events of that dreadful
night of wickedness and retribution which issued in Belshazzar's death, and all accounts which he received would set
Daniel in the fore-front. Nor was this all. The mention of
the part he acted in deciphering the handwriting on the wall
would be invariably connected with the rehearsal of all that
he had done in the reign of Nebuchadnezzar, and of all that
he had been to that great monarch. Most naturally, therefore, would the new emperor desire to avail himself of his
services, the rather that, perhaps, from personal intercourse
with him, he had discovered his talents and abilities; and, as
the best means of securing his assistance and allegiance, he
placed him in the highest position which he had at his dis-
posal. This view of the case is in no degree inconsistent
with the fact that from all accounts Darius was himself a
man given up to sensuality and self-indulgence, since not
unfrequently in history we have instances of princes of that
character who had the discernment to discover, and the wisdom to employ, men of the highest attainments and the
most unswerving integrity.

But it could not be expected that the selection of Daniel
for such a post of distinction would be tamely acquiesced
in by all who were around the court. In particular, the
princes of the kingdoms were filled with envy at the ap-
pointment of the Hebrew, and vowed among themselves to

have him removed as soon as possible. Many reasons
might be assigned for this. For one thing, his age would
be distasteful to them, for Daniel was now advancing toward fourscore years, and they might allege with plausibil-
ity that he was now beyond that time of life when any one
could be expected to discharge with energy and efficiency
the duties of the office with which he had been intrusted.
Then, again, he was a foreigner. He had taken no part in
those campaigns which had created the Medo-Persian Empire, and it might seem to them a crying injustice that the
greatest honor in the new kingdom should be conferred
upon one who had done nothing whatever to assist in its
formation. But, most of all, their enmity would be roused
by the character of Daniel. Had the new vizier been a
man who was likely to wink at their misdeeds, or to share
in their peculations and dishonesties, they might have been
fain to put up with his elevation, and their self-interest
might have held their personal animosity in check; but
when they found that he was distinguished by the highest
principle, and would tolerate no semblance of injustice either toward the subjects on the one hand, or the emperor
on the other, the enmity which they felt on other grounds
was greatly intensified, and they resolved, by fair means or
by foul, to get rid of his supervision. Accordingly, they
scrutinized his conduct through the keen microscope of
malice, if haply they might discover anything on which they
might found an accusation against him. But they soon perceived that all such search was vain, and that if they ever
hoped to circumvent him, it must be in some matter affecting his religion. How honorable all this was to Daniel, I
need hardly stay to remark. It tells us that though he
stood "in that fierce light that beats upon a throne and
blackens every blot," nothing in the least degree degrading
or immoral could be alleged against him; and it tells us,

also, that he made no secret of his religious convictions, but continued, as aforetime, an humble, earnest, and devoted servant of Jehovah. Exaltation has often proved perilous to character. Not every man can stand with unswimming head upon the dizzy height of earthly greatness; not every hand can hold with untrembling steadiness the brimming cup of worldly prosperity. Too often as men become "full," they deny the Lord; and, either because religion is deemed unfashionable, or because they think it stands in the way of their further success, many, who in lowly life have been remarkable for piety, have in the heyday of their social elevation forgotten God, and left their religious convictions in the valley from which they came. But it was not so with Daniel. The same regard to the law of God by which he was distinguished as a youth in the royal college characterized him in the administration of the office of president of the kingdom. His piety was not of that cloistral sort which is hidden from human observation, but it pervaded his life; and so it was that those who came, even in the casual intercourse of official life, into contact with him, felt its influence and were made to confess its power.

In this religion of his, therefore, which his enemies had rightly discovered to be the strongest element of his character, they saw their only hope of undermining him, and they went most insidiously to work to compass his destruction. Insidiously, I said, for they did not openly and manfully accuse him of unfaithfulness to Darius because he was faithful to Jehovah. Had they done that, the king would at once have seen their design, and would have been on his guard against their machinations. But they preferred another course, and came to the monarch, wishing him to enact a law which, in appearance, seemed designed only to honor himself. They pretended that they were deeply solicitous for his glory, and asked him to make a firm decree that whosoever should present a petition to any god or man for thirty days, save to the king himself, should be cast into the den of lions. Such a law, to our Western ears, seems perfectly absurd, and no doubt, as Dr. Pusey says, "religiously viewed, it was extreme insanity;" but, as the same author has affirmed, "that which was in truth insane—to pray to man as if he were God, to neglect God for man—is simple matter of fact. The Persians looked upon their king as the representative of Ormuzd, as indwelt by him, and, as such, gave him divine honors. Persians, Persian monuments, contemporary Greek authors, all attest this. 'With us,' said Artabanus to Themistocles, 'of many and good laws, this is the best—to honor the king, and worship him as the image of God, who preserveth all things.' Curtius says, 'The Persians worship their kings among their gods;' and Isocrates speaks of them as 'worshipping indeed a mortal man, and addressing him as a divine being, but dishonoring the gods more than men.'"* In the light of this fact, then, we can see how the edict proposed by the princes neither shocked Darius nor indicated to him in any way that it had sprung out of a conspiracy against his favorite minister. Much, indeed, might be said by the princes in its behalf. The Babylonians and other provinces had only recently come under his dominion, and they might represent that the object of the decree was to obtain, from these new subjects, special recognition of the king as the representative of the Supreme Power and invested with his delegated authority.

Nor is this all. That the Persians did somehow thus regard their king is evident from the fact so frequently brought before us, both in this history and in that of Esther, that the royal edicts could not be altered. A man claiming to act through a divine prescience could not afford

---

* Pusey's "Lectures," pp. 445, 446.

to appear fallible or changeable; hence, to keep up the fiction of the divinity of royalty, the decrees which issued from him were unalterable.   This being the case, these princes easily prevailed upon the king to do as they wished; and certainly, we who live in an age when a conclave of archbishops and bishops—educated men, in the full blaze of the enlightenment of the nineteenth century—have solemnly issued an edict affirming the infallibility of a fellow-mortal, need not be surprised at the success of these unscrupulous men in a heathen kingdom, some hundreds of years before the birth of Christ.

The penalty suggested by these princes is peculiar, and may be noted as a minute coincidence with ancient history. Had this book been the work of an impostor, then we may be sure that, having already spoken of a burning fiery furnace as having been in Babylon the means of punishing those who refused to worship the golden image which Nebuchadnezzar had set up, the author would again have specified fire as the element of execution.   But this would have been altogether out of keeping with the Medo-Persian custom; for the Medes and Persians were fire-worshippers, and it would have been regarded as impious in the extreme to consign to the sacred flames those who had been guilty either of high treason or of any other crime.   In the omission of fire, therefore, as the penalty of disobedience, we have a coincidence with ancient Persian superstition, which, because it is minute and undesigned, is a valuable witness-bearer to the authenticity of the narrative.   Moreover, we know that it was no uncommon thing among the Persians to consign criminals to wild beasts.   Thus, Bertholdt has said, "The enclosures of wild beasts, especially of lions, which the kings of Asia and North-western Africa formerly had, as they have at the present day, were generally constructed underground, but were ordinarily caves which had been excavated for the purpose, walled up at the sides, and then enclosed within an outer wall, through which a door led from the outer wall to the space within the walls within which persons could pass round and contemplate the wild beasts."*

Such, then, was the proposed decree, with the suggested penalty. We do not hear that Daniel was present either at the concoction of the edict or at the time when it was submitted to the king. If he had been there, he would most probably have protested against it, and from his weight with the monarch might very likely have carried his point. But conspirators so astute as the princes were, would be sure to embrace some opportunity when he was absent from the city; and so, in all probability, Daniel knew nothing about it until, on his return to his residence, he was informed concerning it. But, whensoever or howsoever he first heard of it, he did not require a long time to make up his mind how he would act in the matter. He was pre-eminently a man of decision, and wherever his duty to God was concerned he knew only one course to follow. Indeed, we can scarcely conceive that he deliberated a single moment as to his duty or as to his determination. He would say within himself, " It is not necessary for me to live, and, sooner or later, death will come to me. What does it matter whether it come by the attack of wild beasts or whatever else ? I can die, but I cannot be guilty of such blasphemous idolatry as to pray to Darius as a god ; neither can I allow myself, through the fear of man, to be deprived of the blessed privilege of communion with Jehovah." So he went about his devotions as before, determined to let things otherwise take their course, and casting himself on the gracious help of the Most High.

---

* Barnes's "Commentary," *in loco.*

"He went into his house, and, his windows being open in his chamber toward Jerusalem, he kneeled upon his knees three times a day, and prayed, and gave thanks before his God." Now, at first sight, this looks like ostentation; but when we are fully acquainted with the whole case, we find there was nothing of display about it; for, first, it was the habit of his life to act after this fashion, and had he altered it at that particular time, it would have been said, and with some measure of justice too, that he was afraid of the consequences that would ensue if he continued to do as he had done before. But such a thing would have been disastrous. It would have ruined his character. It would have destroyed his influence, and he had better have died than have lived on to be the contempt and by-word of the heathen for his cowardice and inconsistency. But, second, this mode of procedure which Daniel adopted in his devotions was, for a Jew, perfectly rational and right. He was taught to regard Jerusalem as the city of the Great King. There had been the temple, and the shechinah, and the mercy-seat; and that there was some peculiar significance in turning toward Jerusalem is evident from the fact that even in his dedication prayer at the opening of the temple Solomon refers to it.* No doubt, therefore, the custom up to that time had been to look toward the tabernacle; and if you think a moment or two, you will speedily discover how this came to be the case. In the tabernacle, as afterward in the temple, was the holy of holies, where was the ark, whose lid was sprinkled with the blood of atonement and overshadowed by the wings of the cherubim, between which the symbol of the Divine Presence ever hovered. Now, in turning toward that in prayer, the pious Jew recognized the necessity of propitiation in order to acceptance with God. He

---

* 1 Kings viii., 44-48.

cried to God, not simply as the Supreme Being, but to God as propitiated by sacrifice. He approached him thus as his covenant God through a mediator, which was at the same time a sacrifice. Turning toward Jerusalem, therefore, was to the pious Jew substantially the same thing as approaching God through Christ is now to the Christian. It was the acknowledgment of a mediator and atonement. It was a pleading of atonement; it was to him what the formula "for Christ's sake," when we intelligently use it, is to us. That I am not guilty of over-refining here is clear from the words of Jesus to the woman at the well, in which he plainly intimated that, up till the time at which he spoke, the Jews were right in maintaining that Jerusalem was the place where men ought to worship; but that by his appearance, and from and after the moment when he was speaking, all this was changed, and men now might worship the Father anywhere, provided they worshipped him as Father, and in spirit and in truth.* But why did the appearance of Jesus do away with the localizing of worship at Jerusalem? Because, I answer, he is the mediator and sacrifice of a new covenant, wherein the holy of holies is heaven, and the outer tabernacle earth; so that now men from any portion of the surface of the earth may approach Jehovah, provided only they approach him through Christ. Until Christ came, therefore, the Jews were right in praying toward Jerusalem.

Still, again, Daniel prayed toward Jerusalem to show his faith that the people would yet again possess the holy city. He had the deep conviction that the captivity was ere long to cease, and he would show the strength of his confidence in that future event by looking westward while he made supplication.

---

* John iv., 21–24.

These considerations, therefore, will be enough to show that Daniel could not take refuge in the spirituality of God, or seek to worship him in any other way than he had been accustomed to do.

I am not sure, however, that his devotion was so public as at first we are apt to imagine, for in order to discover him his enemies had to assemble, and the phrase rendered "found Daniel praying" literally implies that they found him after a search, so that they had used means to discover whether or not he obeyed the intolerant enactment. Of course they found him. They knew they would so find him; and right merrily they went to tell the king, chuckling the while over the downfall of their hated president.

When the monarch heard what they had to tell, the full truth for the first time presented itself to his view. He found that he had been cunningly caught in the trap as well as Daniel, for the unchangeability that characterized the Persian laws would not allow him to draw back, and he saw nothing for it but that Daniel must die. And yet what a stupid figment that was to come between him and justice! Even as he yielded to it, one can see that the king was not satisfied with the subterfuge. His conscience told him that he might and could deliver his valued servant; yet, under an alleged necessity, which was no necessity at all, he at length gave him up to the lion's den. No doubt he labored till the going-down of the sun to deliver him. No doubt, also, he was very sad and sorry at all that had transpired; but yet he did the deed, and gave up the best man in his court to the machinations of his enemies.

Ah! how often this has been repeated in history! We think of Herod, who loved John, in a sense, and heard him gladly, and who yet sorrowfully gave him up to the executioner's axe, under the idea that he must keep his promise to a giddy girl, and stand well with the drunken revellers by whom he was surrounded. We think of Pilate, washing his hands before the crowd, as if that would cleanse his heart from the bloody spot by which it was stained when he gave up Jesus to the cross. We think of multitudes in a lower grade of society, who after some deed of drunkenness, or dishonesty, or meanness, shelter themselves behind the subterfuge, that they could not help themselves, because they were under the necessity of doing as they did.

"Under the necessity!" Is not sin an act of the will? and is not the will free? And if the necessity be so great as they represent, why their sorrow and distress? Ah! the conscience will not be thus juggled with; and you may rely upon it that wherever remorse is, there is the inner consciousness that the man could have done otherwise if he had chosen.

We know not whether Daniel was present while the king labored to deliver him; but if he was, he would be saddened by the sight of the monarch's weakness, and might pity his lack of energy and determination.

When Palissy, the Huguenot potter, was lying a prisoner in the Bastile for his adherence to the Protestant faith, it is said that the King of France, who had a great regard for him, visited him in his dungeon, and told him that if he did not comply with the established religion, he should be forced, however unwillingly, to leave him in the hands of his enemies. "Forced, sire!" replied the noble old man, with all the energy and fire of his earlier years; "this is not to speak like a king; but they who force you cannot force me. I can die."

So I doubt not Daniel felt as he went out from the royal presence to be led to the lions' den. True, the king did say as he was going, "Thy God whom thou servest continually, he will deliver thee;" but for all so pious as that speech appears, we are forced to regard it as absurd. He looked

to Providence, forsooth, to undo the wrong which he might
and ought to have himself prevented; but he was not the
last who has acted after this fashion. Ah, how often men
have done wrong to their neighbors, and then piously, or,
rather, impiously and hypocritically, told them to trust God
that all would yet be well! What a mockery of one's misery is this! And how true the words that even "the tender
mercies of the wicked are cruel!"

But Daniel had other thoughts in his heart than for the
king. His spirit was filled with faith. He knew that God
would either sustain him to die for his glory, or deliver him
out of the mouth of the lion, and so he went bravely forward.
And his faith reaped a rich reward; for, although the door
into the den was sealed after Daniel had been thrust into
it, the seal could not keep out the protection of his God,
and so it happened that when the morning dawned, the
king, whose conscience would not let him rest, found that
he was alive. One can imagine the relief which the monarch would feel when he heard his servant's voice, and how
eagerly he would hasten to have him removed from his
place of imprisonment.

But we cannot omit a passing reference to the words of
Daniel, "My God hath sent his angel, and hath shut the
lions' mouths that they have not hurt me." "My God!"
What a familiar confidence there is in these words! "His
angel!" And so Daniel was not without company in the
den of lions. The angel of the covenant, who had been
with his three friends in the furnace, had been his companion. The second person of the blessed Trinity, perhaps
also in human form, had been with him. What holy com-
munings they must have had! what happy fellowship!
There was no music, nor dancing, nor gladness, in the palace of Darius that night; but there was true celestial joy in
the intercourse between Daniel and the angel in the den.

No wonder the lions were subdued into harmlessness. They recognized their Lord, and fawned about his feet or leaped on him in demonstrations of affection, giving him the "lambent homage" of their tongues. As, long after, the winds and waves obeyed him, and cowered down into silence and smoothness on the Lake of Galilee at his word, so now the lions lay in quiet at his feet, while Daniel—like his apocalyptic brother John—lay in affection on his breast.

But we must not linger thus. After Daniel had been taken from the den, the anger of the king was turned upon his persecutors, and he immediately consigned them to the fate which they had intended for their president. As Haman was hanged on the gallows which he had prepared for Mordecai; as, according to the ballad of Southey, Sir Ralph the Rover, who cut away the Inch Cape Bell, perished, with all his crew, upon the Inch Cape Rock; as, according to the general principle which the Psalmist announces, the wicked fall into the pit which they make for others,* so these persecutors were taken in the net which they had woven for Daniel's ensnarement. It is the old story of "vaulting ambition, which o'erleaps itself and falls on th' other side." We do not vindicate the king for the swift vengeance which he took upon them, yet we cannot fail to mark the illustration which it furnishes of the wise man's words, "Whoso diggeth a pit shall fall therein; and he that rolleth a stone, it will return upon him."†

As in the case of Nebuchadnezzar with the three young Hebrews, so now again, in that of Darius with Daniel, this wonderful deliverance was followed by a decree in which the heathen monarch bears testimony to Jehovah's greatness, and calls on all men to tremble and fear before the Lord. But it does not appear that any great change was

---

* Psa. vii., 15, 16; ix., 15, 16.　　　† Prov. xxvi., 27.

wrought by it on Darius himself. He probably imagined that he had done his part when he had published his decree, even as many among ourselves content themselves with words when deeds would be more appropriate. But it is so easy for one to compound with his conscience for his own sins by enforcing duty upon others, that we can well understand his procedure; and it is so common withal that none of us can condemn Darius for it without pronouncing sentence also on himself.

I have to-night endeavored to give a practical tone to my discourse throughout, and so there is the less need for lengthened remarks by way of application. Let the following hints suffice.

We may learn, in the first place, that we must not expect to escape accusation in the world. No matter how carefully we order our lives, slander will have something to say against us. The only perfect character the world has ever seen was defamed as that of a political traitor and a profane blasphemer, and it is sufficient for the servant that he be as his Lord. Has he not prepared us for such a contingency by his own words, "Woe unto you when all men shall speak well of you?" and does not his own history and that of his followers make it evident that the nobler the lives we live, the more venomous and virulent will be the abuse that is heaped upon our heads? The loftiest mountains are most frequently struck by the thunder-bolt; the tallest pines feel most the fury of the blast; and so, as a general rule, the men who are most eminent for usefulness and excellence in the Church are those around whom the nets of accusation are most cunningly woven.

Yet let us not rush too rashly to the conclusion that accusation is an endorsement of excellence. If the occasion of it have been furnished by us, as it was by Daniel, in our devotion to the law of our God, then we may value the opposition of our antagonists as much as we do the confidence of our friends. But if, by our own folly and infatuation, we have given ground for the suspicions that are whispered concerning us; if by the companionships which we have been cherishing, and the habits which we have been practising, we have given color to the charges which are brought against us—then we may not shelter ourselves under the Master's words, or console ourselves with the thought that we are only inheriting the good man's lot. Nay, in such a case, if we are martyrs at all, we are so only to our own folly. That is a part of the whirlwind which they must reap who persist, in the face of all expostulation, in sowing the wind.

Let us see to it, therefore, that when men do speak against us, it shall be for some good that is in us, and not for evil that we have done; for our sincere and steadfast adherence to the morality of the Gospel, and not for inconsistencies of which we have been guilty; for something "concerning the law of our God," and not concerning our conduct with our fellow-men; and then, whatever may come upon us, we may be sure that God will, ere long, bring forth "our righteousness as the light, and our judgment as the noonday." "Who is he that will harm you, if ye be followers of that which is good? But and if ye suffer for righteousness' sake, happy are ye; and be not afraid of their terror, neither be ye troubled. But sanctify the Lord God in your hearts; and be ready always to give an answer to every man that asketh you a reason of the hope that is in you, with meekness and fear: having a good conscience; that, whereas they speak evil of you, as of evil-doers, they may be ashamed that falsely accuse your good conversation in Christ. For it is better, if the will of God be so [that is, if ye are to suffer at all], that you suffer for well-doing than for evil-doing."*

---

* 1 Peter iii., 13–17.

We may learn, in the second place, that when we must either sin or suffer, we ought, without hesitation, to prefer the suffering. There was no shadow of indecision about Daniel here. He took no time to deliberate. He consulted not with flesh and blood. He "held no parley with unmanly fears." He met the edict of the king with a refusal as immediate as it was dignified and firm. He did not go about complaining to this one and that one on the subject. He said little, but he did the more. So ought we to meet all temptations to sin, even though, as in this case, they threaten us with death if we refuse to y eld. True, we are not likely, in this land or in this age, to meet this danger in the form in which it was here encountered by Daniel. But though religious intolerance is at least dormant, if not dead, among us, we must not suppose that the alternative of suffering or sin is never now presented to the soul. The merchant who prefers honest poverty to dishonorable gain ; the workman who braves the tyranny of his class rather than do wrong to his employer ; the capitalist who endures the ostracism of his caste rather than treat his workmen with heartless selfishness ; the orphan girl who prefers a life of hardship and ill-requited industry, with honor and the approbation of the Lord, to one of finery and ease, with dishonor and the loss of self-respect ; the youth who gives up his situation rather than go against his conscience—all have had the same alternative set before them that was faced by Daniel on this memorable occasion. And there is scarcely a day that some similar question has not to be settled by each of us in this assembly.

Now, the easiest way to meet such an emergency is to decide at once, and with firmness, for the right. Deliberation is dangerous. The only safety is in immediate action. Where conscience is concerned, second thoughts are ensnaring ; and if you would keep yourself from sin, you must car-

ry out at once the decision which you feel to be the right
one. Say "No!" to the tempter who seeks so cunningly to
make your temporal interest his ally, as he is attacking your
spiritual welfare. Say it as if you meant it; not with levity
and banter, as if you were indulging in a joke, but grandly,
solemnly, sublimely, as one who knows that the destiny of
his eternity is hanging on its utterance. Say it like Joseph
when he asked, "How can I do this great wickedness, and
sin against God?" Say it like Moses when "he esteemed
the reproach of Christ greater riches than all the treasures
of Egypt." Say it like Nehemiah, when he made reply to
Sanballat, "I am doing a great work, so that I cannot come
down: why should the work cease, whilst I leave it, and
come down to you?" A little word it is, yet everything depends on your saying it in the right way and at the right
time; and those have been the heroes of human history who
have said it most emphatically even in the face of the dungeon and the stake. But you cannot say it thus without
confidence in God. The root of courage is in faith; and
when we shall possess that clear-eyed vision of the invisible
One which sustained Moses in his work and Daniel in his
danger, we shall be at no loss as to the decision we shall
make between sin and suffering. We shall say, "It is not
necessary for me to be free from pain, but it is necessary
for me to keep myself pure; it is not necessary for me to
live any longer on the earth, but while I live it is necessary
that I do right: here I stand, God help me, Amen!" And
though the world may never hear of it, that is heroism as
truly as Daniel's defiance of the edict of Darius, or Luther's
appearance before the Diet of Worms.

Finally, we may learn that no human power can keep us
from prayer. Darius might make a decree that no one
throughout his empire was to ask a petition of any god for
thirty days, but how was he to enforce it? For prayer is

the utterance of the heart to God, and it is as natural to the soul as its cry is to the infant. You may prevent the man from going to the sanctuary; you may even so muzzle him that he cannot articulate a syllable; but when you have done all that, you have not made it impossible for him to pray; for in his secret soul is his true closet, and to that he can retire in spite of all your prohibitions. You may cast him into a dungeon, and load his limbs with chains, and keep him from all manner of communication with his fellow-men; but you cannot, oh! you cannot, prevent him from speaking within his soul to God. And, what is more, and better still, you cannot keep God from coming to him. The door has never yet been forged, the dungeon has never yet been constructed, that can exclude Jehovah from his suffering ones. He found an entrance to Joseph in the prison to which Potiphar had consigned him; to Peter in the dungeon wherein Herod was so jealously guarding him; and to Paul and Silas, in the inmost cell into which they had been thrust. "I can pray, and that is a great thing," said a dying minister to his friend. Yes, it is a great thing, the highest of all our privileges as followers of Jesus; and of that no human power can deprive us! Blessed be God for this good thing which cannot be taken from us! Let us prize it highly, and prove it thoroughly in our times of prosperity and peace, and when trial and adversity come we shall be the better able to appreciate its value.

VIII.

THE VISION OF THE FOUR BEASTS.

DANIEL vii., 1–28.

WITH the seventh chapter a new and entirely distinct section of the Book of Daniel begins. Up till this point, we have a series of scenes in his own personal history or in that of his friends, with but one prophetic vision, introduced incidentally; and even that was not given primarily to him, but to Nebuchadnezzar, while he was merely the agent in its interpretation. From this point on to the close of the book, however, we have a series of predictions under the representation of visions, with only such appended personal incidents as are needed to mark the dates at which the prophecies were given, or the circumstances under which they were communicated.

This is the portion of the book which has evoked most of the antagonism of rationalistic interpreters, and with good reason, at least from their stand-point; for if the genuineness of these chapters be admitted, then the fulfilment of them in after-historical events is, in the case of many of them, so abundantly evident that we must exclaim, "This is the revelation of God." I am aware of the delicacy and difficulty of the work of interpreting prophecy, especially when any part of it is as yet unfulfilled; nevertheless, the fact that so many of these predictions have been already verified seems to demand that some account should be given of them, while, without any dogmatism or any attempt to prophesy on our own account, we may describe the views which are held by different classes of expositors concerning those sections of them which are as yet waiting their accomplishment.   For myself, I may say that I have never had so deeply impressed upon me the truth of the divine origin of Holy Scripture as when I was studying these chapters ; and if I can succeed in communicating, by the help of God's Spirit, that impression to you, my labor will be abundantly rewarded.   Let us go forward, therefore, confidently, but at the same time cautiously ; and when we approach the confines of the unfulfilled, let us pause and wait, that God in history may interpret God in prophecy.

The vision in this seventh chapter is commonly, and I think correctly, regarded as referring to the same general features of history as that given to Nebuchadnezzar, and described in the second chapter.   Between the two, however, there is this notable distinction — namely, that while Nebuchadnezzar saw the earthly kingdoms, or the world-powers, under the representation of a colossal but lifeless image of a man, the prophet has them portrayed to him under the representation of living animals.   Now, as Auberlen, with true Christian insight, has said, " The outward political history had been shown in general features to the worldly ruler ; for by his position he was peculiarly and almost exclusively fitted to receive a revelation of this kind. But the prophet obtains more minute disclosures, especially on the spiritual and religious character of the powers of the world, and such as were best adapted to *his* position and *his* receptivity.   This difference of character in the revelation easily explains the difference of images.   While in the second chapter they are taken from the sphere of the inanimate, which has only an external side, they are chosen in the seventh chapter from the sphere of the animate.   Further, as Nebuchadnezzar saw things only from without, the world-power appeared to him in its glory as a splendid human figure, and the kingdom of God in its humility as a stone; at first, he beheld the world-power more glorious than the kingdom of God. Daniel, on the other hand, to whom it was given to penetrate further into the inner essence of things, saw that the kingdoms of the world, notwithstanding their defiant power, are of a nature animal, and lower than human; that their minds are estranged from and even opposed to God, and that only in the kingdom of God is the true dignity of humanity revealed; and, accordingly, the kingdom of God appears to him from the outset, and in the very selection of images, superior to the kingdom of this world..... The colossal figure that Nebuchadnezzar beheld represents mankind in its own strength and greatness; but, however splendid, it presents only the outward appearance of a man. But Daniel, regarding mankind in its spiritual condition, saw humanity through its alienation from God degraded to the level of reasonless animals, enslaved by the dark powers of nature. It is only in the kingdom of God that man gains his humanity and destiny; it is only from on high that the living perfect Son of man has come."*

In the first year of Belshazzar our prophet had a vision, in which he saw the sea raging under the violence of a storm, and as he looked there arose out of the waters, one after another, four strange composite animals, over which, as he gazed, certain wonderful transformations passed. Then, after the fourth animal, he saw the Ancient of Days clad in white raiment and seated on a fiery throne; around him were thousands that ministered unto him, and ten thousand times ten thousand stood before him; "the judgment was set, and the books were opened." The beast was slain, and his body was given to the fire, and one like unto "the Son

---

* "Daniel and the Revelation," by Carl August Auberlen; translated by Adolph Saphir, pp. 35, 36.

of man" came with the clouds of heaven, and received dominion and glory and a kingdom, that all people, nations,
and languages should serve him.

The sight of these things greatly troubled Daniel, so that
he made application to one of those that stood around the
throne for the interpretation, and received this reply, which
lays down the principles which every expounder of the vision must follow: "These great beasts, which are four, are
four kings, which shall arise out of the earth. But the saints
of the Most High shall take the kingdom, and possess the
kingdom for ever, even for ever and ever."

These four beasts, then, as we learn, were the representa-
tions of four kingdoms. "The first was like a lion, and had
eagle's wings;"* and while the prophet looked, its wings
"were plucked, and it was lifted from the earth, and made
to stand upon the feet as a man, and a man's heart was
given to it." This is evidently a symbol of the Babylonian
Empire, which had the strength of the lion combined with
the swiftness of the eagle. Jeremiah† has in his prophecies
likened Nebuchadnezzar to both of these animals; and
Ezekiel has compared the king,‡ while Habakkuk§ and Jeremiah had likened his armies, to the eagle.

The changes which passed over this animal as Daniel
looked upon it represent the decay of the Babylonian monarchy. It was made to stand on the feet as a man—that is,
in lieu of the quickness of motion, like eagle's wings, there
was given the slowness of human feet. Its rapidity of conquest was stopped; its savage strength was taken away.
It was weakened and crippled, until at length, as we lately

---

* It is hardly necessary to remind the reader that the Babylonian
sculptures disinterred in recent years make us familiar with such combi-
nations as those described in this vision.

† Jer. iv., 7; Lam. iv., 19.   ‡ Ezek. xvii., 3.   § Hab. i., 8.

saw, in a single night, and almost without striking a blow, its capital was taken by the Medes and Persians.

The second beast was like a bear, and "it raised up itself on one side, and it had three ribs in the mouth of it between the teeth of it: and they said thus unto it, Arise, devour much flesh." This represents the Medo-Persian Empire, and corresponds to the breast and arms of Nebuchadnezzar's image. As in the man the right arm is stronger than the left, so the bear is raised up on one side. The bear moves awkwardly, and so, in contrast with the winged rapidity of the Chaldean conquests, the Persian advances were slow and heavy. The "three ribs" in its mouth correspond accurately to the three kingdoms which the Medo-Persian Empire swallowed up, namely, the Lydian, Babylonian, and Egyptian; and the command given to it, "Arise, devour much flesh," may indicate that still other kingdoms were to be absorbed by it, while at the same time it may suggest, that waste of human life which was a characteristic of the Persian Empire in its heavy aggressiveness.*

The third beast was "like a leopard," or panther, "which had upon the back of it four wings of a fowl; the beast had also four heads; and dominion was given to it." This is designed to represent the Grecian Empire; first, in its unity under Alexander the Great, and, second, in its division into four monarchies under his four generals. The panther is remarkable for swiftness; and Alexander was as rapid as he was daring in his conquests. The leopard is of small size, but of great courage, and is not afraid to encounter the largest beasts of the forest; so Alexander, a little king in comparison, of small stature too, and with a small army, dared to attack the king of kings, that is, the mon-

---

* This is fully established by Pusey in his "Lectures on Daniel the Prophet," p. 70.

arch of Persia, whose kingdom extended from the Ægean
Sea to the Indies. The subdivision of the empire is indicated by its four heads; and probably also the number of
heads may be a symbol of circumspection and manifold, ver-
satile intelligence.

The fourth beast has no name given to it, but is described
as "dreadful and terrible, and strong exceedingly; and it
had great iron teeth: it devoured and brake in pieces, and
stamped the residue with the feet of it: and it was diverse
from all the beasts that were before it, and it had ten horns;"
and while the prophet considered the horns, "there came
up among them another little horn, before whom there were
three of the first horns plucked up by the roots: and, behold, in this horn were eyes like the eyes of man, and a mouth
speaking great things." This last symbol seems most to
have affected the prophet's mind. It contained in it more
than he had learned from the explanation of the "legs of
iron and clay" in Nebuchadnezzar's image, and the following interpretation of its meaning was, at his earnest request,
vouchsafed to him: "The fourth beast shall be the fourth
kingdom upon earth, which shall be diverse from all kingdoms, and shall devour the whole earth, and shall tread it
down, and break it in pieces. And the ten horns out of this
kingdom are ten kings that shall arise; and another shall
rise after them; and he shall be diverse from the first,
and he shall subdue three kings. And he shall speak great
words against the Most High, and shall wear out the saints
of the Most High, and think to change times and laws: and
they shall be given into his hand until a time and times"
(that is, two times, for the word is dual) "and the dividing
of time. But the judgment shall sit, and they shall take
away his dominion, to consume and to destroy it unto the
end."

Now, concerning this beast and the explanation here given of the changes that passed upon it, there has been much controversy among commentators. I shall content myself with putting before you the principal opinions. Some have supposed that this animal represents the Grecian Empire after Alexander's death; that the ten horns are ten kings of different sections of it; and that the little horn is Antiochus Epiphanes. But against this view we have to set the fact that the vision here runs parallel to that of Nebuchadnezzar's image, which, as we saw when we were considering it, is most naturally understood of the Babylonian, Persian, Grecian, and Roman kingdoms.

Again, the kingdom of the Seleucidæ is always regarded as a part of the great Greek Empire, and never spoken of as being in itself a new one. Once more, in the leopard with its four heads we have already had the Grecian Empire as a whole, and it is not natural to regard it as set before us in one of its sections only in this fourth animal. Still further, in Antiochus Epiphanes there was nothing diverse, in kind at least, from other kings. His peculiar distinction was not that he was of a different sort from others, but only that he was worse; and so, though there are certainly in his reign some marvellous coincidences with the statements made regarding this little horn, we cannot view him as meeting all the requirements of the case. For these reasons, a large number of expositors are in favor of regarding this animal as representing the Roman Empire.

But even among those who adopt this general idea there are distinct differences. They may be divided into three classes. The first, of whom Calvin may be named as a specimen, find the ten horns in the number of separate kingdoms of which the Roman Empire was composed. They suppose that the little horn means Julius Cæsar; and the overthrow of the whole they discover in the first advent of the Messiah, when he came to found that spiritual king-

dom which is yet destined to be universal and everlasting.
To this interpretation, however, there are insuperable objections; for the ten horns are said to be kings or kingdoms rising out of that which is symbolized by the beast,
and cannot, therefore, be taken as meaning the different
parts of which, as a whole, it was originally composed. As
the four heads of the leopard represented the partition of
Alexander's kingdom, so the ten horns of this beast must
represent a partition of the kingdom denoted by the beast.
Again, there was nothing in Julius Cæsar diverse from other
earthly potentates.   No doubt, he had astuteness and ability and military skill in a larger measure than almost any
other general; but these were the same in kind as those
possessed by others, the only difference being in degree.
Therefore, this interpretation does not meet the full requirements of the case.

The great preponderance of opinion among commentators, therefore, is in favor of what may be called the papal
interpretation; and without in any way indicating my preference for it, I shall endeavor to set it vividly before you as
it is given by the most prominent of this class of authors.
In the view of these writers, then, the fourth beast represents the Roman Empire. "It was so great and horrible
that it was not easy to find an adequate name for it; and
the Roman Empire was dreadful and terrible and strong
exceedingly, beyond any of the former kingdoms. It was
diverse from all kingdoms, not only in its republican form
of government, but likewise in strength and power and
greatness, and duration and extent of dominion. It devoured, and brake in pieces, and stamped the residue with
the feet of it; it reduced Macedonia into a Roman province, about 168 B.C.; the kingdom of Pergamus, about 133
B.C.; Syria, about 65 B.C.; and Egypt, about 30 B.C. And
besides the remains of the Macedonian Empire, it subdued

many other provinces and kingdoms; so that it might, by a very usual figure, be said to devour the whole earth, and to tread it down, and to break it in pieces, and become, in a manner, what the Roman writers delighted to call it, ' *terrarum orbis imperium*,' the empire of the whole world."* The ten horns of the beast are the ten kingdoms which constituted, at the fall of the Roman Empire, what Bishop Newton has called "the broken pieces," into which it was cut up, and which, according to Machiavel,† who was not thinking of Daniel when he made the enumeration, were these ten: the Ostrogoths, the Visigoths, the Swenes and Alans, the Vandals, the Franks, the Burgundians, the Heruli and Turingi, the Saxons, the Huns, and the Lombards. Other enumerations have been given by Mede, by Lloyd, by Sir Isaac Newton, etc.; and some have supposed that the numeral ten stands here simply as a definite for an indefinite number.

The "little horn" spoken of in verse 8th is regarded by this class of interpreters as the Bishop of Rome when he became a temporal prince. "The Bishop of Rome," says Bishop Newton,‡ "was respectable as a bishop long before; but he did not become 'a horn' properly, which is an emblem of strength and power, till he became 'a temporal prince.' He was to rise after the others, that is, behind them, and, as Mede explains it, so that the kings were not aware of the growing-up of the little horn till it overtopped them." Three of the first horns—that is, three of the first kings or kingdoms—were to be plucked up by the roots and to fall before it. And these three, according to Sir Isaac Newton, were; first, the exarchate of Ravenna, which of right

---

* "Dissertations on the Prophecies," by Thomas Newton, D.D., sometime Lord Bishop of Bristol, p. 230.

† Ibid., p. 232.   ‡ Ibid., p. 241.

belonged to the Greek emperors, and was given to Pope Stephen II. by Pepin, because his predecessor had acknowledged him, though a usurper, to be the lawful sovereign of France. This was effected about the year 755. Second, the kingdom of the Lombards, which was often troublesome to the popes, so that at the instigation of one of the pontiffs, Charlemagne, successor of Pepin, came with a great army, and conquered it, and gave a great part of it to the Holy See. This was in the year 774. Third, the city and dukedom of Rome, which was made over by the same Charlemagne to Leo III.

Other authors have given a slightly different enumeration ; but all this class of interpreters are careful to remark that the Pope has in a manner designated himself as the person indicated by wearing the tiara, or triple crown. In other respects, too, the Pope, in their view, fully answers the character of the little horn. It was to be diverse from the first, and so the power of the popes is, or rather was, unlike that of other princes, being ecclesiastical as well as temporal. In this horn were "eyes like the eyes of man," to denote, they say, cunning and foresight—his looking out and watching for all opportunities to promote his own interest ; and with this agrees the policy of the Roman hierarchy, which, as they say, has almost passed into a proverb for these peculiarities.

"He had a mouth, speaking very great things ;" and who, they ask, hath been more noisy and blustering than the Pope, boasting of his supremacy, thundering with his anathemas, bellowing with his bulls, excommunicating princes, absolving subjects from their allegiance, and claiming even the infallibility of God ?

"And he shall speak great words against the Most High ;" and who, again, they ask, has so set himself up above all laws, human and divine, arrogating to himself godlike attributes and titles of holiness and infallibility, insulting men and blaspheming God, as the Pope has?

"And he shall wear out the saints of the Most High;" that is, as they affirm, he shall waste God's people by wars, Inquisitions, persecutions, massacres, and the like; and we must admit that the papacy may well deserve to be so described.

"And he shall think to change times and laws," appointing fasts and feasts, canonizing saints, granting pardons for sin and indulgences to sin, instituting new modes of worship, imposing new articles of faith, enjoining new rules of practice, such as celibacy, and reversing at pleasure the laws of God and man. No doubt this, also, may be said with truth of the papacy.

"And they shall be given into his hands for a time, two times, and the dividing of time." A time, all this class of interpreters agree, is a year. So a time, two times, and half a time make three years and a half. Now, taking the computation of a day for a year, which, without any warrant, they always take, and reckoning a month at thirty days, we get the forty and two months of Revelation (xi., 2), and the twelve hundred and sixty days of Revelation (xi., 3, and xii., 6). This kingdom of the papacy, therefore, which is temporal and spiritual, is to last, so say these interpreters, for twelve hundred and sixty years.

But much difference of opinion has been entertained among them as to the period from which the calculation is to be made. Some would reckon it from the issuing of the edict of Justinian acknowledging the Pope to be the head of the Church, A.D. 533; others would take it from the decree of Phocas, by which the title of Justinian was confirmed, and of which the date is A.D. 606; others count it from the grant of Pepin of the kingdom of Lombardy, by which the Pope first became a temporal monarch, the date of which

is A.D. 752. The second of these dates was that adopted
by Robert Fleming, in his work on the "Rise and Fall of
the Papacy," first published in 1701, wherein he says, "If
we may suppose that Antichrist began his reign in the year
606, the additional twelve hundred and sixty years, were they
Julian or ordinary years, would lead down to 1866 ; but, seeing they are prophetical years of only three hundred and
sixty days, we must cast away eighteen years, and thus the
final period of the papal usurpation must conclude in 1848."
This was the statement that was so frequently quoted, as
those of us then old enough to take note of what was said
will remember, in that memorable year when the Pope was
compelled to become a fugitive from Rome ; and it was certainly a striking coincidence. Elliot, in his "Horæ Apoca-
lypticæ," dates from the edict of Justinian, 529 to 533, and
adding 1260 to these we have 1789 to 1793, the era of the
first French Revolution, when certainly the papacy received
the first of that series of blows from which it is still reeling,
and from which it will probably never recover. Others,
however, take the date from 754, and tell us we are not to
expect the downfall of Antichrist till the year 2014.

I have given these different interpretations more as a
matter of curiosity than because I am willing to endorse
any one of them. For such investigations as these, I confess I have little taste, and though many singular coincidences have occurred, I own that I shrink from descending
to such particulars, and perilling the argument which may
be drawn from the prophecy as a whole on the accuracy of
a single date.

But we must hasten on. This kingdom and the little horn
rising out of it are to be destroyed at length by the power
of the Son of man, a name which here we meet in prophecy
for the first time. Heaven is opened to us as to the prophet. We see the throne, and the Ancient of Days seated

thereon. The judgment is set, and the books are opened; and one like unto the Son of man is there, like man, but not a mere man; man, but more than man; and to him is given power, and glory, and kingdom, that all peoples should serve him, and his dominion is to last forever. We know this Son of man; and we know, too, that as in the case of the destruction of Jerusalem, his coming, here foretold, is not that of a personal presence, but rather of a providential judgment and a great ingathering of souls to himself.

The whole description of verses 13 and 14 is but, as it were, a dramatizing of the words of the Second Psalm: "Ask of me, and I shall give thee the heathen for thine inheritance, and the uttermost parts of the earth for thy possession." And so the end shall come: might is not always to prevail, truth is yet to come uppermost. The flock of Christ is not always to be feeble and small, but the earth shall be filled with his knowledge as the waters cover the sea. "He shall reign till all his enemies are put under him." His name is "King of kings and Lord of lords," and the day is coming when the shout shall be heard on high, "Hallelujah! the kingdoms of the world are become the kingdoms of our Lord and of his Christ." As surely as the truth of this vision in regard to the three first kingdoms has been demonstrated, so surely shall it be made manifest by the destruction of the fourth, with its little horn, of vanity, and blasphemy, and cruelty, and in the setting-up of a great, spiritual, universal, and eternal kingdom, with Jesus sitting supreme on the throne of loving and loyal human hearts.

But now, leaving the subject of the interpretation of this remarkable prophecy, let us attempt to get at the practical and permanent principles which underlie it, and which are at once profoundly suggestive and exceedingly important.

Foremost among these, we find the terribly significant truth that earthly power in and of itself degenerates into brutality. The appropriate symbol of a great empire is a wild beast. From the day when Nimrod founded Babel on till that when the latest empire that has been added to the list of the world's monarchies was consummated, the kingdoms of the earth have stood on military conquest. Might has taken the place of right. The weakest has been driven to the wall, and the cruelties which have been practised on the battle-field and in connection with victory have given the fullest illustration of the poet's words, "Man's inhumanity to man makes countless thousands mourn." The sword has been the arbiter of imperial dynasties, and the struggles between rival powers have been as fierce and destructive as the contentions of wild animals in the jungle. Nay, even in our own century, the age of peace societies, and international conferences, and exhibitions of the products of industry to which the civilized world has been asked to contribute, we have seen again and again that resort has been had to war for the settlement of differences between neighboring states. We all exclaim against the brutality of the prize-fight, wherein two men consent to beat each other into bruised and bleeding flesh for the paltry consideration of a sum of money or the empty honor of a championship. But what better is it when armies seek to annihilate each other for the sake of an addition to national territory, or for the vindication of what is called national honor? The rifle may be a more scientific weapon than the fist, but they are both the instruments of violence; and it is a libel on the intelligence of our humanity, not to say also on the Christianity of our age, to say that no other means can be devised for the settlement of the disputes or the removal of the jealousies that may spring up between different nations.

The Washington treaty is a new thing in international

politics, and it is not by accident that this has been carried
through by the two most thoroughly Christianized nations
on the earth.   Nor ought it to be forgotten in this connection that the English Cabinet under whose auspices, on the
one side at least, that arbitration was agreed on and conducted, had in it more men of earnest personal Christian
convictions than any government which Great Britain has
seen in its history.   When I repeat the names of Gladstone,
Bright, Hatherley, Argyll, it will be at once recognized that
they are those of men who stand in the fore-front of religious thinkers, as well as in the vanguard of a political
party; and when I affirm, as I do on the fullest evidence,
that no man's words on this side of the Atlantic were so in-
fluential in regard to the inauguration of the same treaty
as those of the venerable Christian scholar and philosopher
Theodore Woolsey, you will recognize how much of the un-
worldly element there was in it all.   But that, unhappily, is
still an exceptional case; and the war between France and
Germany a few years ago, as well as that between Russia
and Turkey to-day, is a conclusive proof that among the
world-powers might is still supreme, while the barbarities
which have been reported in the latter instance with, I fear,
too much truth, on both sides, attest that the symbolism of
Daniel is as appropriate now as it was in the time of Belshazzar.   Alas! who can think of all this without joining
the recluse of Olney in his lament, as through the "loop-
hole" of his retreat he sighs,

> "Oh for a lodge in some vast wilderness,
>   Some boundless contiguity of shade,
>   Where rumor of oppression and deceit,
>   Of unsuccessful or successful war,
>   Might never reach me more! My ear is pain'd,
>   My soul is sick with every day's report
>   Of wrong and outrage with which earth is fill'd:

> There is no flesh in man's obdurate heart;
> It does not bleed for man; the natural bond
> Of brotherhood is sever'd as the flax
> That falls asunder at the touch of fire."*

But observe, again, that the tendency of this brutality is to increase. The four beasts that Daniel saw came in this order: first the lion, then the bear, then the panther, then that huge composite, unnamed, almost unnamable, animal, with "great iron teeth, devouring and breaking in pieces, and stamping the residue with the feet of it." We have heard a great deal lately of theories of development, and this is neither the place nor the time to enter upon the consideration of these so far as they seek to explain the physical universe; but, morally, the only development of man, when left to himself, which history has seen, has been downward. Bad as the Babylonians were, they were outdone by the Persians; and these were exceeded by the Greeks; while the Romans were worst of all.

Let it be noted, also, that all this while the nations were growing in what has been called culture and civilization. The art and poetry and philosophy of Greece have never been excelled; and Rome was the heir of the highest civilization that had gone before it. But, after all, that was merely a superficial thing, and served only very thinly to veneer the rottenness and cruelty which were beneath. You may suspect my testimony; but if you accept that of Mr. Lecky, in his "History of Morals," he will tell you that Greece was a mass of reeking corruption; and Mr. Anthony Trollope has given us a most harrowing description of Roman cruelty, which, from its bearing on the very point before us, I must take the liberty of quoting. He says, "That which will most strike the ordinary English reader

---

* Cowper's "Task," Book II.

in the narrative of Cæsar is the cruelty of the Romans —
cruelty of which Cæsar himself is guilty to a frightful extent, and of which he never expresses horror. And yet
among his contemporaries he achieved a character for clem-
ency which he has retained to this day. In describing the
character of Cæsar without reference to that of his contemporaries, it is impossible not to declare him to have been
terribly cruel. From blood-thirstiness he slaughtered none,
but neither from tenderness did he spare any. *All was done
from policy; and when policy seemed to demand blood he could
without a scruple—as far as we can judge, without a pang—
order the destruction of human beings, having no regard to number, sex, age, innocence, or helplessness.* Our only excuse for
him is that he was a Roman, and that Romans were indifferent to blood. Suicide was with them the common mode
of avoiding otherwise inevitable misfortune; and it was natural that men who made light of their own lives should
make light of the lives of others. Of all those with whose
names the reader will become acquainted in the following
pages " (" The Commentaries of Cæsar "), " hardly one or two
died in their beds." Then, having amply proved that statement, he goes on to say, " The bloody catalogue is so complete, so nearly comprises all whose names are mentioned,
that it strikes the reader with almost a comic horror. But
when we come to *the slaughter of whole towns; to the devas-
tation of country effected purposely that men and women might
starve; to the abandonment of the old, the young, and the tender, that they might perish on the hill-sides; to the mutilation
of crowds of men; to the burning of cities told us in a passing
word; to the drowning of many thousands—mentioned as we
should mention the destruction of a brood of rats*—the comedy
is all over, and the heart becomes sick. Then it is we remember that the coming of Christ has changed all things,
and that men now—though terrible things have been done

since Christ came to us—are not as men were in the days
of Cæsar."* Nothing needs to be added to this statement
in order to prove the brutality of the power symbolized by
this fourth beast, save to say that the history of the development of the Empire in later days, as traced by Gibbon,
contains the record of even greater enormities, if that be
possible, than those of which Cæsar was guilty.

But if this be so, then we are prepared for the third lesson suggested by this prophecy — namely, that the restoration of man to humanity must come, not from himself, but
from above. He who introduced the healing salt which is
yet to purify thoroughly the bitter fountain of our earthly
life was sent forth from "the Ancient of Days." He came
from heaven to earth, that he might elevate earth at length
to heaven. He, the "Son of God," became the "Son of
man," that he might make us sons of God. Had he been a
man and no more, he could not have arrested the downward
moral development that was in progress. But because he
was God incarnate, because he came from above, he is able
to introduce an antidote to the corruption of our human
nature.

There are few more striking arguments for the divine
origin of the Gospel, and the deity of its author, than that
which may be drawn from the contrast between the character of Jesus and that of his age. Recall the words of Trollope which I have just quoted, or lift such a work, for example, as Forsyth's "Life of Cicero," and see what a sink of
iniquity and corruption Rome had become only a few years
before the birth of Christ. Peruse the writings of Josephus,
and mark how he describes in blackest characters the im-

* "The Commentaries of Cæsar," by Anthony Trollope, in the "Series of Ancient Classics for English Readers," pp. 24–27. The italics are
our own.

morality of the Jewish people in the days of Herod the Great. Then take the four Gospels and read them, and you will perceive that the difference between them is not one of degree, but of nature. By what process of "evolution" could Jesus Christ have been produced out of such an age? Consider the attributes of character by which he was distinguished. His meekness and humility were equalled only by his honesty and benevolence. There was about him a conscientious thoroughness, which was carried out at every sacrifice; and so far from having that love of ostentation which might have been expected in a deceiver, there was in him a disposition rather to check the impulsive ardor of those who wished to blaze abroad the glory of his power. His Sermon on the Mount evinces that, beyond all other things in religion, he delighted in truth in the inward parts, and held in abhorrence that cold and hollow ritualism which is content with "the form of godliness," while "denying its power." Never was there such an equipoise of moral attributes as we find in him. To an all-embracing love he joined a sternness of principle which exposed wrong wherever he found it, and insisted on faithfulness even in that which is least. With the humility of a child, there was combined in him the sublime self-consciousness of one who "thought it not robbery to be equal with God;" and with the tenderness of a woman there was associated the courage of a hero. But most of all, pervading his other qualities, and shedding its own bright halo round them all, was his self-sacrificing and devoted LOVE. Before the portrait which these evangelists have painted, men of every age have stood in rooted admiration; and the influence of his life and death and teachings has put the benevolence into our modern life. If it has not yet succeeded in destroying war, it has sent its ministers of mercy to the battle-field, to care for the wounded and soothe the dying; and by-and-by, under the teaching of his Spirit, men shall "beat their swords into ploughshares, and their spears into pruning-hooks."

Now, do not tell me that such a character was the natural outgrowth of his times. Take Rome before the Advent, with Cicero as a representative of its philosophy and statesmanship, Horace as the popular idol among its poets, and Anthony as a specimen of its morals; take the philosophy of Greece, with its different sects of Stoics, Epicureans, Platonists, and the like; take Judaism, whether as seen at Alexandria among the disciples of Philo, or in Judea among the formal Pharisees, the sceptical Sadducees, or the ascetic Essenes. Put all these into the crucible of such an age as that undeniably was, and by what amalgam known to men could these elements have produced Jesus Christ? Christ the outgrowth of his age? No! The legitimate child of such an age was the dilettante *littérateur*, the amateur musician, the fashionable charioteer, the inhuman monster, Nero! But, so far from being a development of his generation, Jesus was crucified by his generation for being what he was; and the inscription over his cross, written as it was in letters of Greek and Latin and Hebrew, may fitly symbolize the agreement of all the three nationalities in putting him to death. He was no development of his age, but, instead, everything true and noble and loving and godlike in succeeding generations has been a development of him; and when men, standing around his cross, shall learn to combine in their lives obedience to the precepts of his Sermon on the Mount with the reception of the principle that pervades his parable of the Good Samaritan, then will be the return of that golden age to which the poets of antiquity looked so wistfully back, and the beginning of that millennium which Christians are so prayerfully expecting.

Thus, then, the hope of the world lies in the diffusion of the Gospel of Christ, and to us, in this age and in this land,

the high privilege has been given of laboring in this holy
and benevolent enterprise.   The truth as it is in Jesus is
the great purifier and elevator of human society.   Civilization without the Gospel is, as we have seen, only a veneered
brutality.   But wherever the Gospel goes in power, it re-
stores men to humanity by bringing them back to God.
Man was made in the image of his Creator, and so the
purest godlikeness will ever be the truest humanity.   But
to have godlikeness we must have God's Son dwelling in
us ; and when we have attained that blessing, we shall not
seek to keep it to ourselves, but shall work, and pray, and
give, that others may share it with us.   To this bloodless
crusade let me summon you now ; for when the Church of
Christ shall go forth in earnest as a missionary of love to
the nations, she will be the most effective Peace Society ;
and, in the proportion in which men embrace the principles
of the Saviour, cruelty will disappear from the earth.   Let
us give ourselves, beloved brethren, to this holy enterprise,
and we shall thus help on the coming of the day when
the prophecy shall be fulfilled — a prophecy so much more
significant in our eyes, after our consideration of the symbolism of this vision of Daniel, "The wolf also shall dwell
with the lamb, and the leopard shall lie down with the kid ;
and the calf and the young lion and the fatling together ;
and a little child shall lead them.   And the cow and the
bear shall feed ; their young ones shall lie down together :
and the lion shall eat straw like the ox."* May the Lord
hasten it in its time !

* Isa. xi., 6, 7.

IX.

VISION OF THE RAM AND THE HE-GOAT.

DANIEL viii., 1–27.

TWO years after Daniel had seen the vision so minutely described in our last lecture, and while he was residing at Shushan, which was afterward the summer palace of the Persian monarchs, there came to him another supernatural revelation, which fitted into, and filled in, the outline which had been given in the former in regard at least to two of the great world-powers.

He saw two hostile animals, one a ram, and the other a he-goat, contending with each other, and after the ram had been destroyed, the great horn which he had marked between the eyes of the goat was broken, and four horns came out upon its forehead. Then out of one of these a little horn came forth, which waxed great, and magnified itself against the worship of the Most High. While the prophet was looking on the vision, he heard a colloquy between two holy ones, from which he received the information that the little horn was to be triumphant for two thousand and three hundred days; and at the close of all, when he was seeking for the meaning of the vision, there stood before him the appearance of a man, who called to Gabriel, saying, "Make this man to understand the vision." This the angel did, in simple but significant words, and the effect upon the prophet was so great that he fainted and was sick certain days. Thus we are not left to conjecture the interpretation of this singular vision, for just as, in the parables of the sower and the tares, the Saviour has given the key to their meaning, so here the explanations furnished by Gabriel lay down the lines which we must follow.   Let us therefore advance under this celestial guidance to the investigation of the prophecy.

The ram which Daniel saw was the Persian Empire.   The two horns were the two kingdoms of Media and Persia of which it was composed.   The one horn higher than the other which came up last was the Persian monarchy, which, though latest in developing its strength, did ultimately, in the reign of Cyrus, overtop, and indeed almost absorb, Media.   "The ram pushed westward, and northward, and southward; so that no beasts might stand before him, neither was there any that could deliver out of his hand; but he did according to his will, and became great."   So the conquests of the Persians are described.   Nothing is said of their doings eastward; but they subdued, westward, Babylon, Mesopotamia, Syria, and Asia Minor; southward, Palestine, with parts of Egypt, Arabia, and Ethiopia; and northward, Colchis, Armenia, and the regions around the Caspian Sea. Such was the power of this empire, that for a long time it was acknowledged to be the foremost in the world, and it met with no successful opposition until it was confronted with the forces of Greece at Marathon, Salamis, and Platæa.

"The rough goat is the king of Grecia: and the great horn that is between his eyes is the first king."   Thus the goat, so long as the one horn continued unbroken, symbolized the Macedonian Empire in its first form as united under one monarch; and it is interesting to note that the symbol of a goat is often found in various ways in connection with Macedonia, and was used as an emblem of that kingdom.   Of this custom a mythological origin is furnished in the statement that Caramus, the first king of Macedonia, was led by goats to the site where he established the capital of his kingdom. Mr. Combe, writing to the editor of "Cal-met's Dictionary," says, in a passage quoted by Mr. Barnes in his commentary on this chapter, "Not only many of the individual towns in Macedon and Thrace employed this type, but the kingdom of Macedonia itself was represented by a goat which had this peculiarity, that it had but one horn." The same author refers to one of the pilasters of Persepolis, on which there seems to be a record of the Macedonians becoming tributary to the Persians in the shape of a goat with an immense horn growing out of the middle of its forehead, while a man dressed like a Persian is standing by its side, and holding the horn with his left hand.

This goat "came from the west on the face of the whole earth, and touched not the ground: * * * * and there was no power in the ram to stand before him, but he cast him down to the ground and stamped upon him: and there was none that could deliver him out of his hands." No symbolism could more expressively or graphically portray the collision between the Greek and Persian empires which resulted in the undisputed sovereignty of Alexander the Great. That great military genius was remarkable for the rapidity of his movements. He came, as it were, flying to victory; so that it might well be said that the goat "touched not the ground." The same characteristic of this general was set before us in the former vision by the union of the wings of a bird to the body of the leopard; and a very slight acquaintance with ancient history is necessary for the appreciation of this vivid picture. We have only to take into consideration a few of the dates of Alexander's life to recognize its accuracy. He was chosen generalissimo of the Greeks against the Persians while yet he was only twenty-one years old; and he died the victim of intemperance at the early age of thirty-three; so that the whole series of his campaigns and victories was comprised within twelve years.   In the year 334 B.C., he crossed the Hellespont, and defeated his enemies on the bank of the Granicus; in 333 B.C., he overthrew Darius at Issus; in 332 B.C., he conquered Tyre and Egypt, and founded the city of Alexandria; in 331 B.C., he crossed the Euphrates and the Tigris and met with the immense hosts of Darius, said to have amounted to more than a million of men, and completely defeated them in the plains of Gaugamela.   Thus in four years he made the entire realm of Persia tributary to Greece.   In 327 B.C., he invaded India, and crossed the Indus, probably near the modern Attock.   Thus in little more than six years he pushed his dominion to the farthest east.

The description of the first shock of conflict between the goat and the ram given in the seventh verse recalls to every one familiar with ancient history the incidents of the battle on the banks of the Granicus, in which the Persians sustained their first defeat at Alexander's hands.   Darius and his army, numbering 100,000 foot and 10,000 horse, occupied the farther side of the river; and the Greeks, who were only 35,000 strong, plunged into the stream, swam across, and rushed on the Persian forces with such fury that, with a loss of barely 100 men, they left 20,000 of the enemy dead upon the field.   This marvellous success spread abroad the terror of the conqueror's name, and prepared the way for his annexation of India.

But his greatness was not to be of long continuance, for though the he-goat waxed strong, the great horn was broken in the very hour of his strength; and "for it came up four notable ones toward the four winds of heaven."   Very melancholy is the closing chapter of the great conqueror's career, and I cannot describe it better than in the following paragraphs from a very unpretentious but really valuable work: "Alexander projected the conquest of India, firmly persuaded that the gods had decreed to him the sovereignty of the whole habitable globe. He penetrated to the Ganges, and would have advanced to the Eastern ocean, had the spirit of his army kept pace with his ambition. But his troops, seeing no end to their toils, refused to proceed. He returned to the Indus, from whence, sending round his fleet to the Persian Gulf, he marched his army across the desert to Persepolis. Indignant that he had found a limit to his conquests, he abandoned himself to every excess of luxury and debauchery. The arrogance of his nature, and the ardor of his passions, heightened by continual intemperance, broke out into the most outrageous excesses of cruelty, for which, in the few intervals of sober reflection, his ingenuous mind suffered the keenest remorse. From Persepolis he returned to Babylon, and there died, after a fit of debauch, in the thirty-third year of his age and thirteenth of his reign. On his death-bed he named no successor, but gave his ring to Perdiccas, one of his officers. When his courtiers asked him to whom he wished the empire to devolve, he replied, 'To the most worthy.' Perdiccas, sensible that his pretensions would not justify a direct assumption of the government of this vast empire, brought about a division of the whole among thirty-three of the principal officers, to each of whom he assigned the charge of a province, and to himself he reserved the commander-in-chiefship of the army, trusting to their inevitable dissensions for an opportunity to reduce them all under his own authority. Hence arose a series of wars and intrigues of which the detail is barren and uninteresting. It is sufficient to say, the consequence was a total extirpation of the family of Alexander, and a new partition of the empire into four great monarchies : Macedon, with a part of Greece, which fell to the share of Canander ; Thrace, Bithynia, and the Northern regions, which were the lot of Lysimachus ; Egypt, with Cyrene and Cyprus, which were the share of Ptolemy; and Syria, with all Upper Asia and the Eastern provinces, which formed the kingdom of Seleucia."* These were the four horns on the head of the goat, and correspond also to the four heads of the leopard in the former vision.

Soon, however, attention is concentrated on the history of one of these divisions, for thus the record proceeds (verses 9–12): "And out of one of them came forth a little horn, which waxed exceeding great, toward the south, and toward the east, and toward the pleasant land. And it waxed great, even to the host of heaven; and it cast down some of the host and of the stars to the ground, and stamped upon them. Yea, he magnified himself even to the prince of the host, and by him the daily sacrifice was taken away, and the place of his sanctuary was cast down. And a host was given him against the daily sacrifice by reason of transgression, and it cast down the truth to the ground; and it practised, and prospered." But with this description we must combine the interpretation given by Gabriel (verses 22–25): "Now that being broken, whereas four stood up for it, four kingdoms shall stand up out' of the nation, but not in his power. And in the latter time of their kingdom, when the transgressors are come to the full, a king of fierce countenance, and understanding dark sentences, shall stand up. And his power shall be mighty, but not by his own power: and he shall destroy wonderfully, and shall prosper, and practise, and shall destroy the mighty and the holy people. And through his policy also he shall cause craft to prosper in his hand; and he shall magnify himself in his heart, and by peace shall destroy many: he shall also stand up against the Prince of princes; but he shall be broken without hand."

---

* "Elements of General History, Ancient and Modern," by Alexander Fraser Tytler, Lord Woodhouselee, pp. 56–58.

In seeking to expound these verses, we must have regard in the outset to the distinction between the "little horn" in this vision and that in the prediction of the seventh chapter. In the latter case, the little horn arose among the ten horns on the head of the fourth beast, which must, as we think, be interpreted of the Roman Empire. But in the vision now before us, the "little horn" springs out of one of the four horns on the head of the goat; that is, out of one of the four kingdoms into which the Grecian Empire was divided after Alexander's death; and "in the latter time" of these kingdoms; that is, just before they were all superseded by the Roman power. Now, if we keep this distinction clearly before us, it will save us from much of the confusion into which expositors have fallen in treating of this chapter. Thus there are many, of whom the excellent Bishop Newton may be cited as a specimen, who take this little horn to represent the Roman Empire as a persecuting power. He says, "The persecuting power of Rome, whether exercised toward the Jews or toward the Christians, by the emperors or by the popes, is still the little horn. The tyranny is the same; but as exerted in Greece and the East, it is the little horn of the he-goat of the third empire; as exerted in Italy and the West, it is the little horn of the fourth beast, or the fourth empire.* But this is to substitute an idealized principle for a concrete kingdom; and in the explanation of Gabriel, the horns are spoken of as representing not abstract qualities, but visible monarchies. We must adhere to that throughout, and therefore we cannot accept the theory which sees in the little horn simply the representative of religious intolerance. There are only two beasts in this vision. Evidently, therefore, the prophecy is restricted to the histories of two out of the four great em-

---

* "Dissertations on the Prophecies," p. 287.

pires to which we have so often alluded; and it is alleged
by Gabriel that these two are the Persian Empire and the
Greek Empire; first, in its united form under Alexander;
and, second, in its divided form, under his four successors.
Now, out of one of these four sections of Alexander's empire some special development was to come "in the latter
time of their kingdom;" and to take that as describing
something which occurred under the Roman Empire, by
which all the four were absorbed, seems to me absurd.
Rather must we look for the fulfilment of this prediction in
some great forth-putting of blasphemous pretension, and
some terrible season of persecution, in one of the divisions
of the Greek Empire, not long before it was overcome by the
power of Rome.   We cannot, therefore, regard this prophecy
as referring to anything that occurred in Roman history.

For a similar reason, we cannot accept the interpretation
of those who see in the little horn of this vision a representation of the rise and progress of Mohammedanism.   This
horn is a development out of one of the four divisions into
which the Greek Empire was broken up, and before they
were destroyed by the fourth world-power.

Still less can we look with favor on the theory of Dr. S. P.
Tregelles on the subject.   That eminent critic looks upon
the appearance of this horn as indicating something that is
still in the future.   He affirms that it is to arise in one of
the four divisions of the empire that was once held by Alexander, and then goes on to allege that "from the mention
of the daily sacrifice and the sanctuary, it is plain that as
part of the actings of the horn these things will be found in
existence: a portion of the Jews will have returned in unbelief to their own land, and the worship of God will be attempted to be carried on according to the Mosaic ritual."*

---

* "Remarks on the Prophetic Visions in the Book of Daniel," by
S. P. Tregelles, p. 94.

But there is nothing of all this in the words of Gabriel; and nothing can be more evident than that we are shut up to a date near that of the close of the four divisions of Alexander's empire, and before the full development of the Roman power. This seems to indicate that the reference is to Antiochus Epiphanes.

That monarch, who was the son of Antiochus the Great, succeeded his brother Seleucus Philopater, and reigned over Syria from 176 B.C. to 164 B.C. He was a brutal tyrant, and proved himself one of the most blood-thirsty enemies of the Jewish nation. He called himself, indeed, Epiphanes, or the Illustrious, but he was frequently styled by others Epimanes, or the Maniac. Many of his evil deeds are related in the books of the Maccabees, and the merest summary of these, which is all that we can now attempt to give, will be sufficient to identify him with the little horn of this vision. In his youth he had been given by his father as a hostage to the Romans, but was released by the kindness of his brother, who sent his own son in his stead. In the same year his brother was murdered by one Heliodorus, who seized upon the throne, but was speedily dispossessed by Antiochus. His sister, Cleopatra, who had been married to the King of Egypt, having died, Antiochus laid claim to Cœlesyria and Palestine, and this led to a war with Egypt, wherein "he waxed great toward the south." It was during this war that he perpetrated those cruelties upon the Jews—the inhabitants of "the pleasant land"—which have made his name forever infamous to the chosen people, and which gave rise to those heroic strivings for independence with which the history of Judas Maccabæus is imperishably associated.

While Antiochus was in Egypt seeking to conquer that country, a false rumor of his death was circulated throughout Palestine, and filled the peoples' hearts with joy, be-

cause by his influence the true high-priest had been thrust
out of his office, to make way for an unprincipled man who
was one of his own creatures.   When he was informed of
the satisfaction with which the news of his reported death
had been received by the Jews, and especially of the attempt made by the rightful high-priest to regain his position, he chose to believe that the entire Jewish nation had
revolted; and, marching with all haste, he laid siege to Jerusalem and took it, slaying in three days more than forty
thousand persons, and taking as many more captives, to be
sold as slaves.   Not content with this, he forced his way
into the Temple, entered the very holy of holies itself, and
caused a great sow to be offered in sacrifice upon the altar
of burnt-offering, while broth made from the same unclean
flesh was sprinkled by his order over the sacred precincts
for the purpose of defiling them.   On his departure, he took
with him the altar of incense, the golden candlestick, the
table of showbread, and other sacred vessels, to the value
of eighteen hundred talents of gold.   He established in the
office of high-priest the traitor Menelaus, who had been his
conductor into the Temple, and left behind him a Phrygian
named Philip, a man of cruel and barbarous disposition, to
be governor of Jerusalem.

Two years after the commission of these enormities, returning from another invasion of Egypt, where he had been
checkmated by the Romans, he vented his disappointment
upon the Jews, and detailed from his army twenty-two thousand men, under Apollonius, with orders to destroy Jerusalem.   On his arrival at the holy city, Apollonius conducted
himself peaceably, concealing his purpose till the Sabbath;
but on that day, when the people were assembled in their
synagogues, he let loose his soldiers upon them, and commanded them to slay all the men, but to take captive all the
women and children.   These orders were only too faithfully

obeyed, so that the streets were filled with blood. He
spoiled the city of its treasures, set fire to it in several
places, pulled down the walls, and, with the materials so
obtained, erected a fortress on an eminence in the city of
David over against the Temple, and thoroughly commanding its courts. From this stronghold the soldiers fell on all
who went up to worship; and, as a consequence, the Temple was deserted, and the daily sacrifices ceased to be offered. I ought to mention also that the statue of Jupiter
Olympus was introduced into the Temple, and victims offered to it on the altar of Jehovah. In connection with these
enormities, proclamations were issued forbidding circumcis-
ion, enjoining the eating of all manner of unclean meats,
and commanding the profanation of the Sabbath and festival days. From Jerusalem the persecution spread over the
land; and, "as a last insult, the feasts of the Bacchanalia,
the license of which, as they were celebrated in the later
ages of Greece, shocked the severe virtue of the older Romans, were substituted for the national festival of Taberna-
cles."* Thus the sad description in the seventy-ninth
Psalm was verified: "O God, the heathen are come into
thine inheritance; thy holy temple have they defiled; they
have laid Jerusalem on heaps. The dead bodies of thy
servants have they given to be meat unto the fowls of the
heaven, the flesh of thy saints unto the beasts of the earth.
Their blood have they shed like water round about Jerusalem; and there was none to bury them. We are become a
reproach to our neighbors, a scorn and derision to them
that are round about us." And those who take note of the
fearful cruelties to which they were subjected will not wonder at the prayer which follows: "Pour out thy wrath upon
the heathen that have not known thee, and upon the kingdoms that have not called upon thy name."

---

* Milman's "History of the Jews," vol. ii., pp. 38–44.

In the vision before us, it is said that "a host was given him against the daily sacrifice by reason of transgression;" and in Gabriel's explanation the appearance of this king of fierce countenance is dated in "the latter time of their kingdom, when the transgressors are come to the full." We may conclude, therefore, that all this came upon the Jewish people, as a chastisement for their sins; and perhaps the historian of the Maccabees gives us the explanation of these clauses when he says, "In those days went there out of Israel wicked men, who persuaded many, saying, Let us go and make covenant with the heathen that are round about us; for since we departed from them we have had much sorrow. So this device pleased them well. Then certain of the people were so forward herein, that they went to the king, who gave them license to do after the ordinances of the heathen, whereupon they built a place of exercise at Jerusalem, according to the custom of the heathen, and made themselves uncircumcised, and forsook the holy covenant and joined themselves to the heathen, and were sold to do mischief."*

But the desolation of the sanctuary, though thus, as it seems probable, designed to reprove the conformity of the Jews to heathen customs, was not to be perpetual. The altars were to be restored. The sacrifices were again to be offered daily in the Temple court; for "many in Israel were fully resolved, and confirmed in themselves, not to carry out the ordinances of Antiochus in the eating of unclean things; wherefore they chose rather to die, that they might not profane the holy covenant."† Among these faithful ones were Mattathias and his sons, who, with some others, fled to the wilderness, where they remained until they gained an opportunity of taking up arms for themselves and their country.

---

* 1 Macc. i., 11-15.   † Ibid. i., 62, 63.

After a series of the bravest struggles and the most brilliant triumphs, which flame forth as redeeming features in the later history of the Jewish nation, Judas Maccabæus, with his followers, entered the ruined Jerusalem. He found shrubs growing in the courts of the Temple, and the chambers of the priests thrown down. "With wild lamentations and the sound of martial trumpets, they mingled their prayers and praises to the God of their fathers. Judas took the precaution to keep a body of armed men on the watch against the Syrian garrison in the citadel, and then proceeded to install the most blameless of the priests in their office, to repair the sacred edifice, purify every part from the profanation of the heathen, construct a new altar, and replace out of the booty all the sacred vessels.* This he did with such demonstration of gladness, that, in commemoration of the restoration of worship in their sanctuary, the Jews established an annual festival, which was kept for eight days, and called the Feast of the Dedication.†

In connection with this restoration of the daily sacrifice, however, the only serious difficulty rising out of the interpretation which we have given of this prophecy emerges. Josephus has alleged that the Temple was cleansed just three years and six months after the setting-up of the statue of Jupiter Olympus in the Holy of Holies.‡ Now, three and a half years, taking three hundred and sixty days for a year, will give twelve hundred and sixty days; whereas in the conversation between the two holy ones (verses 13, 14) it is said that these desolations were to last two thousand three hundred days. But presuming that the precise number is given, and not merely a definite for an indefinite number, the

---

* Milman's "History of the Jews," vol. ii., p. 52.
† See John x., 22 ; 1 Macc. iv., 36–59.
‡ Josephus, "Wars of the Jews," I., i., 1.

discrepancy may be thus accounted for.   The vision may include the whole line of events beginning with the siege of
Jerusalem by Antiochus, while Josephus may be restricting
his calculation to the precise interval between the setting-up
of the statue of Jupiter in the Temple and the restoration
of the daily sacrifices.   This is the view taken by Calvin
on the subject, for he says: "Two thousand three hundred
days fill up six years and three months and a half.   Now,
if we compare the testimony of history, and especially of the
Book of Maccabees, with this prophecy, we shall find that
miserable race oppressed for six years under the tyranny of
Antiochus.   The idol of Olympian Jupiter did not remain
in the Temple for six continuous years, but the commencement of the pollution occurred at the very first attack, as if
he would insult the very face of God.   As, therefore, religion was then laid prostrate on the ground until the cleans-
ing of the Temple, we see how very clearly the prophecy
and the history agree, as far as this narrative is concerned."

It only remains that we refer for a moment to the death
of Antiochus, which is described in the words of Gabriel:
"He shall be broken without hand."   Returning from an
unsuccessful expedition against Persia, he died in a small
town among the mountains of Paretacene, not by violence,
but by a strange disease, loathsome almost as that by which
Herod was smitten in the moment of his blasphemy.*   But
the pain of his body was not to be compared to the anguish
of his spirit, for he was afflicted by horrible apparitions and
remorse, the consequence, as the historian of the Maccabees
asserts, of his barbarity and sacrilege in Judea.†

But wherein, it may be asked, was the necessity for thus
predicting these enormities, and the destruction of him who
should inflict them?   The obvious answer is because An-

---

* Acts xii., 23.   † See the whole description, 1 Macc. vi., 1–16.

tiochus confronted the people of God with a danger which
never before had menaced them, and the Lord thus gra-
ciously designed to furnish them beforehand with special
grace by which they might be sustained.   None of the
world - powers by whom the Jews had been subjugated up
till this time had interfered to any great extent with their
worship.   On the contrary, as we learn from many passages
in this Book of Daniel, and in those of Ezra and Nehemiah,
they had been protected in their religion, and had even been
assisted by heathen emperors in rebuilding their Temple.
But now one was about to appear who would endeavor to
destroy their religion altogether, and it was necessary that
they should be forewarned of his attacks, tha they might
be forearmed to meet them.   Nothing in the whole former
history of Israel can be compared with the sufferings which
the people endured at the hands of Antiochus ; and the
fruit which this prophecy bore was the glorious struggle of
the Maccabees, which gave a new lustre to the Jewish name.

I have left myself little time for any extended practical
remarks, but I may not conclude without gleaning a few lessons for our modern life from the volume of history which
is outlined in this remarkable vision.

We may learn, then, in the first place, that the strength
of one evil habit may overcome even the mightiest conquer-
or.   Very suggestive, in this regard, is the history of Alexander the Great ; and it is not without a sigh of regret that
we read of the pupil of the famous Aristotle dying as the
victim of his own excesses at the early age of thirty-three.
He could conquer the world by his armies, yet intemperance was his master and destroyer.   He was filled with
rage and disappointment because he was foiled in his efforts
to reach the Eastern Ocean, yet was he never fired with the
nobler ambition of overmastering the world within himself.
He had the greatness of taking not cities only, but empires ;

yet he knew nothing of the higher greatness of ruling his own spirit; and the contrast between his life and that of Another which lasted only three-and-thirty years cannot but strike every thoughtful reader of ancient history.

But how many there are, even among ourselves, who have made similar conquests, and been themselves similarly overcome! We think of those two poets, the one a peer, and the other a ploughman, who won for themselves the crown which is awarded only to the rarest genius, and yet were held by the chains of ignominious and debasing habit. We think of the merchant who has acquired ample fortune, outdistancing all competitors, but falls at last into a drunkard's grave. We think of the workman whose energy and skill have placed him in the front rank of inventors, but who lived in thirsty wretchedness, a meaner man than multitudes who had not half his ingenuity. We think of the youth who has gained for himself the affection of his circle, and is the idol of his family and his neighborhood, but sinks at length into rags and reproach, because he has become the slave of the bottle. It would almost seem that the dreadful habit of intemperance has a peculiar affinity for the sensitive organizations of those who are cut out for special excellence in some department of human activity. The eloquent orator; the entrancing musician; the poet with his frenzied eye and burning words; the man with that special magnetism that attracts the affection of every one to himself; in a word, the possessor of that subtle thing which we call genius, seems to be in particular danger from strong drink; and not unfrequently reputations that would be otherwise irreproachable are blurred and blotted by intemperance.

The world has become wiser in many respects since Alexander's days, but in this it has made little progress; and we may be forgiven, therefore, if we seek to point a moral from the great Grecian emperor's excesses. To no purpose

shall we gain other crowns, if we are ourselves the slaves of
appetite. .The most splendid education, and the most unpar-
alleled successes in other respects, will not compensate for
the ruin of character; and, standing here at the grave of
Alexander, we renew our warning against the deceitfulness
of strong drink.   It is easier to acquire a habit than it is to
break it off; so let me urge every one who is starting out
on the battle of life to wage his first warfare with himself.
Settle at the very outset the question whether you are to be
the body's, or your body is to be yours; and see to it that
you do not advance to the great work of your existence
handicapped and hampered by an evil habit.   Resolve that
appetite shall never overmaster you; and remember that
when you have vanquished self, you are already a mightier
conqueror than was the great Alexander after he had subdued the world.

We may learn, in the second place, that conformity to
the world is fraught with great danger to the people of God.
If we have been right in conjecturing that the evils which
came upon the Jews in the days of Antiochus were designed
as chastisements for their unfaithfulness to the covenant,
the history over which we have come is, in this regard, full
of most salutary warning.   Nor does it stand alone.   The
same lesson comes out of every chapter of the Book of
Judges, and is most solemnly enforced by the captivity of
the Hebrews in the Babylonish land.   And though the sanctions of the ancient covenant were mainly national and temporal, let no one imagine that these disciplinary chastisements which came upon the Jews have no meaning for us
in these New Testament days; for the peculiar excellences
of the Christian's character are his truest safeguards in the
world.   Read, again, the last chapter of the Epistle to the
Ephesians, and you will see that the Christian's graces are,
at the same time, his armor.   If, therefore, we would keep

ourselves in safety from the fiery darts of the wicked one, we must cultivate those peculiarities of the Christian character which are the very *raison d'être* of its existence. The tendency of these days, indeed, is to minimize the difference between the Christian and other men ; and the boundary between the Church and the world, which in the Word of God, is as clearly defined as the lines of latitude and longitude on the map, is in actual life almost as imperceptible as are these lines upon the surface of the globe. So it happens that the Church of Christ is invaded by the unbelieving, and its power to resist and overcome the world is thereby sadly weakened. That which gives salt all its value is its saltness ; and when that quality is lost by it, men cast it from them and trample it underfoot. Its wholesome character and antiseptic influence depend upon its peculiarity ; and when that is lost, it is useless. In the same way, our peculiarities as Christians are the very elements of our power. By these it is that the Church has its aggressive force and purifying influence upon the world ; and when these are lost, then we may look for some avenging Antiochus to menace its very existence on the earth. So long as the Church maintains its character as a witness-bearer for Christ, and for that truth and that integrity which he has enjoined, God will keep it strong and prosperous ; but when it falls below its mission, and sinks into a mere empty formalism, be sure that Antiochus is at the door !

Nor should we fail to mark the bearing of these principles on our national history. By the great favor of our God, this republic has been permitted to enter upon the second century of its life, and many eloquent eulogiums have been pronounced on those who fought the battles of its early independence. But let us never forget that it is to be conserved by the same qualities as those by which it was gained. Imitation is the grandest panegyric ; and the noblest centennial oration will be to follow the example of the fathers of the republic. We cannot, indeed, be the mere repetition of them; and to attempt to produce anything of that kind would be as ridiculous as it would be for us to go back to the fashion of their dress. But we can imbibe their principles, and apply these to the evils of our times as courageously as they applied them to the circumstances of their age. They were distinguished by honesty, temperance, truth, patriotism, and piety; and concerning these qualities we may say, as the barons of Runnymede said of their swords, " By these we have obtained our liberties, and with these we will defend them." Let us act on their principles in our conflict with internal corruption, with the same fidelity and disinterestedness as they did in their resistance to external oppression, and the second century of our history will be even more glorious than the first; but if we fall from these, be sure that some Antiochus will come to rifle us of our treasures, and make our high places desolate!

We may learn, finally, the limited power of the enemies of God's people. The spoliation of Jerusalem by Antiochus was to be only for a season. The world-tyrant could go only a certain length. Like Satan with Job, he was under a divine restraint, which said to him, " Hitherto shalt thou come, and no farther." God is stronger than the mightiest man; and so to the people of God who continue faithful unto him there is a limit of calamity. The longest night is followed by the dawn; and, as the proverb has it, " Time and the hour run through the roughest day." Trial will not always last; and the prediction which to-night we have been considering was given to Daniel, that it might sustain the people under new and unheard-of suffering, by the prospect of a speedy relief. Inspired by the truth which was here declared, Judas and his faithful band " were strong, and did exploits." They knew that God was on their side; and

though the ordeal was tremendous, they clung fast to him.
Nay, the very severity of the conflict developed in them a
courage that was akin to that of the greatest of their fathers.
So let us bear up under all calamity, in the spirit of him
who said, " Our light affliction, which is but for a moment,
worketh for us a far more exceeding and eternal weight of
glory. While we look not at the things which are seen,
but at the things which are unseen; for the things which
are seen are temporal, but the things which are unseen are
eternal." Be patient, be uncompromising, be courageous.
" Stablish your hearts, for the coming of the Lord draweth
nigh." It is but a little while, and then we shall enter the
new Jerusalem, with more triumphant ecstasy than the
great Maccabæus felt when he stood in the courts of the old
Temple ; and

> " When the shore is won at last,
> Who shall count the billows past ?"

X.

THE SEVENTY WEEKS.

DANIEL ix., 1–27.

THOUGH Daniel's hands were filled with the business of the king whom he served, his heart was ever turned toward Jerusalem. This was not simply because that city was the metropolis of his father-land, but rather because it was the "place which God had chosen to place his name there." The patriotism of the Jew was rooted in his piety; and though Jerusalem was dear to him for the beauty of its situation, and for the stirring associations which clustered round its heights, it was especially sacred in his estimation as "the city of God."

So long, therefore, as it was in ruins, and its Temple lying waste, Daniel could not but be sad, and, deep down beneath all other desires in his soul, there was the longing for the time when Jehovah would return and visit "the vineyard which his right hand had planted, and the branch which he had made strong for himself." In the time of his worldly prosperity, the state of Jerusalem was ever present to his mind to give deep shadings to his happiness; while, in the day of his adversity, the tears which he shed over his own sorrows were not so bitter as those which he wept when he remembered Zion. Even amidst the splendors of Shushan, Nehemiah had great "sorrow of heart," when he heard the tidings which his kinsman brought concerning "the city of their solemnities;" and we do not wonder that Daniel also was greatly exercised about the condition of the Jewish peo-

ple, and the cause of God with which they were so identified. These subjects, indeed, were never, we may believe,
entirely absent from his thoughts. No doubt he gave himself diligently to the discharge of the duties of his office ;
but behind his usual occupations, and forming, so to say,
the inner chamber of his life, to which in moments of leisure he constantly retired, was the great question, "O God,
how long shall the adversary reproach? shall the enemy
blaspheme thy name forever?"*

As the years revolved with, to mere human view, no
clearer prospects of improvement, the burden became so
heavy that he gave himself to special prayer for the city
which was called by God's name. More than sixty years
had gone since the day when, as a boy, he had been taken
from Jerusalem and carried off to Babylon. The burden
of fourscore years was now upon him, and he must soon
"go the way of all the earth ;" but his heart was yearning
for the revival of God's work, which to him centred in the
recovery of their own land by the chosen people. So in the
first year of Darius he devoted a season to fasting and
prayer, for the coming of the time "when God should arise
and have mercy upon Zion."

It is interesting to mark that this devotional fervor of
Daniel grew out of his study of the Word of God. Reading the prophecies of Jeremiah, he found such passages as
these : "This whole land shall be a desolation, and an astonishment ; and these nations shall serve the king of Babylon seventy years ;" and, again, "After seventy years be
accomplished at Babylon, I will visit you, and perform my
good word toward you in causing you to return to this
place."† Now, as he had been himself for nearly seventy
years a captive, he felt assured that, no matter from what

---

* Psa. lxxiv., 10. † Jer. xxv., 11 ; xxix., 10.

particular time the beginning of the Captivity proper might
be dated, its termination was drawing near, and he set himself to pray to God concerning it.   At first sight, this seems
strange.   God gives a prediction by the mouth of Jeremiah ;
Daniel discovers it, and believes it, and then prays for its
fulfilment.   Could he not have left God to accomplish his
own prophecy, without troubling him with any prayer ?   So
reasons the man who believes neither in God, nor in prophecy, nor in prayer.   But the heart of the child has an in-
stinct which is truer than all logic, and when he gets a promise he turns it at once into a prayer.   Every parent knows
how true that is in his intercourse with his own children, for
when he has set a time for the bestowment of a particular
gift, the nearer the day approaches, the more frequently he
is reminded of his pledge.   Can that, therefore, be ridiculous in a child of God which is so natural and so touching
in our own offspring ?

Nor let any one imagine that in pleading for the fulfilment of God's prophecies or promises—for every promise
is a species of prophecy—we are doing an unnecessary
thing, for beneath each of his gracious utterances there is
this condition, "for this will I be inquired of them to do it
for them ;" and he who has ordained the end has also ordained prayer as one of the means by which the end is to
be gained.   Indeed, God was beginning to fulfil his prophecy given by Jeremiah when he stirred up Daniel to pray
about it ; and whensoever we see a spirit of supplication
poured out upon a people, we may take that as an indication that God has begun to prepare them for receiving the
accomplishment of some promise of blessing.   The belief
that the blessing will certainly come is a stimulus, rather
than a hinderance, to prayer.   When I receive a check
from a fellow-man, I am not deterred from presenting it at
the bank because I know that the money is sure to be forth-

coming. Nay, I am only thereby the more encouraged to take it and turn it into money. But the same thing holds good when we take God's promises and present them at the throne of grace. It is not because we do not believe in them or in him that we ask for their fulfilment, but rather because we do put implicit trust in them both; and the firmer our faith is, the more earnest will be our supplication.

The prayer offered by Daniel on this occasion is remarkable for its simplicity, its fervor, and its appropriateness. Its introductory portion consists mainly of confession, and in that exercise, identifying himself with the nation to which he belonged, he acknowledges the guilt of Israel in former days, and admits the justness of the punishment which had been inflicted on them for their iniquities. Then referring to that great primal deliverance from Egypt by which God manifested his special interest in the children of Abraham, he pleads, by implication, the ancient covenant, and earnestly begs that God would cause his face to shine upon his sanctuary. He is careful, also, to add that he presents his supplications, not on the ground of his own righteousness, or that of the people, but for God's great mercies. We cannot but be struck with the Scriptural ground on which this prayer rests, the straightforward honesty by which its confessions are characterized, the utter absence of self-righteousness by which it is distinguished, and the fervent importunity with which it concludes; but, as I have elsewhere dwelt on these things,* I press on to look at the answer which was given to its request.

While Daniel was engaged in his devotions, the same celestial one who had explained to him his former vision appeared to him, and informed him that he was sent to give him skill and understanding, and to show him yet more

---

* See "Prayer and Business," Randolph & Co., New York.

fully concerning things to come, because he was a "man
greatly beloved." Truly "the secret of the Lord is with
them that fear him; and he will show them his covenant."*
Herein also we may see an instance of the fulfilment of the
promise, "It shall come to pass, that before they call, I will
answer; and while they are yet speaking, I will hear."†
At the very commencement of his supplications this heavenly messenger was commissioned to repair to him, "being
caused to fly swiftly," and just as his petitions were ended
he breaks in with the answer. We must beware, however,
of drawing from this statement inferences which it will not
warrant. It does not imply, either that the angels have
wings, and move through space by flying, or that the whole
time during which Daniel was praying was required by Gabriel for coming from heaven to earth. It simply means
that the angel came promptly, like as a man comes who
is breathless and weary with quick running. But that he
needed all this time to pass from heaven to earth I do not
myself suppose. The boundary between the earthly and
the heavenly is not so much one of distance as of nature.
For anything that we can tell, the spiritual is all around us.
True, we teach our children to sing of the "happy land" as
"far, far away;" but I have never been able to accept that
representation as Scriptural; and to me no place is nearer
than the realm of spirits. I cannot cross the street without
taking some time in which to do it, but I may be with God
in a moment. The Christian apostle has taught us that "to
depart" is to be "with Christ," and that absence from the
body is presence with the Lord. So it is not distance that
separates us from the spirit land. Now, if these principles
be just, we must take the statement here as figurative, and
regard the marks as if of haste, which Gabriel bore, as de-

---

* Psa. xxv., 14.   † Isa. lxv., 24.

signed to give to Daniel the assurance that God was deeply
interested in him, and eager to relieve his anxiety. At least
they furnish no warrant for attempting, as some have done,
to calculate the distance of heaven from earth, or speculat-
ing, as others have done, on the mode in which the ministry of angels is carried on; for everything savoring of ma-
terialism must be eliminated from our consideration of such
a subject.

The great thing we learn here is the reality of the ministry of angels. The miracle was not in the fact that Gabriel
was there, but rather in his being made visible to Daniel;
just as when Elisha was in Dothan, the miracle was not in
the presence of God's hosts round about the prophet, but in
the opening of the young man's eyes, so that he saw them.
God commonly employs his angels as his messengers; and
if we are his children, and the heirs of his salvation, they
have often ministered to us when we knew it not; but their
help was not the less real, because at the moment of their
rendering it they were not perceived by us. In a home
which I know well, a mother, before retiring for the night,
went her rounds through the bedrooms of her children, making them comfortable in their cots. One she tucked carefully in; another she lifted and made more easy on his pil-
low; a third she cooled by throwing off the heavy coverlet
by which she was oppressed; and when she came down
again to her own chamber she said to her husband, "Dear
unconscious ones! they never knew that I was near them."
But her ministry was real and beneficial, notwithstanding
their unconsciousness. So it is, save in exceptional cases,
with the ministrations of those angelic attendants whom
God has commissioned to wait upon his people. They gird
us when we know it not. They soothe us when we think
not of it; and as on the other side of the veil, they give
their report to their Master, they too may say, "Blessed

souls! they did not know that we had been near them."
How much God is always doing for us that we know nothing of at the moment! And among these unconscious blessings that we are always receiving at his hands, I number the
ministry of angels.

> "O the exceeding grace
> Of highest God, that loves his creatures so,
> And all his works with mercy doth embrace,
> That blessed angels he sends to and fro
> To serve to wicked men, to serve his wicked foe!
> How oft do they their silken bowers leave,
> To come to succor us that succor want!
> How oft do they with golden pinions cleave
> The flitting skies, like flying pursuivant,
> Against foul fiends to aid us militant!
> They for us fight, they watch and duly ward,
> And their bright squadrons round about us plant;
> And all for love, and nothing for reward.
> Oh, why should heavenly God to man have such regard!"*

But we must look now at the new revelation made to
Daniel by Gabriel. It is given as an answer to his prayer;
and yet, when we inspect it narrowly, we discover that the
great subject of his anxiety is referred to in it only by implication. He asked about God's sanctuary, and the reply
refers to events which presuppose that the Temple must be
restored, and Jerusalem rebuilt. He made a request which
was founded on his discovery of Jeremiah's prediction that
the Captivity should continue seventy years, and the answer
assures him that for the one seventy in exile, there should
be seven seventies of continued occupation of the holy city
by the Jews. It is plain, therefore, that the reference of the
angel's words throughout is to years. The "heptades" are
not weeks of days; but as Daniel from the beginning was

---

* Spenser.

exercised about the seventy years, the seventy sevens must be understood of the same denomination. We are not, therefore, taking a day for a year when we interpret these "heptades" as consisting each of seven years. So far as we have been able to discover, the day for a year theory, as it is called, has no foundation in the Word of God, and we are anxious, at the outset of our interpretation of this prediction, to guard against being understood as indorsing any such fanciful and fictitious views.

In the words of Gabriel, these seventy heptades are spoken of, first, generally; then he gives us an account of certain marked epochs in them ; and finally he presents us with a foreshadowing of what was to happen at their close. Let us glance a little at each of these divisions of the prophecy.

The first is given in the twenty-fourth verse ; but, as the English reader may perceive, from the unusual number of marginal emendations, that it is difficult to render the original with exactness, it may be well to give the rendering which is now preferred by the best Hebrew scholars. I select that of Dr. Cowles.* "Seventy sevens [of years] are determined in reference to thy people and thy holy city, to shut up sin, to seal transgression, to cover iniquity, to bring in everlasting righteousness, to seal up vision and prophet, and to anoint the Holy of Holies." The phrases "to shut up sin, to seal transgression, to cover iniquity," describe most appropriately the sacrificial character and sanctifying influence of the death of Christ, as these are set before us in the New Testament. The expressions "to bring in everlasting righteousness," and "to seal up vision and prophet," refer, as interpreted by the fuller light of the apostolic epistles, to the work of Christ as furnishing his people with an everlast-

---

* "Ezekiel and Daniel, with Notes," by Henry Cowles, D.D., p. 401.

ing righteousness, and sealing up, by fulfilling the prophecies of God; for "the testimony of Jesus is the spirit of
prophecy." The anointing of the Holy of Holies is by
some referred to the purification of the literal Temple by
the presence in it of Incarnate God; but to me it seems
rather to describe the descent of the Holy Spirit on the Son
of God, whose body was called by himself a temple. So
far, then, as this verse is concerned, it declares that in some
way, and from some date, four hundred and ninety years
were to run their course before the work by which sin should
be expiated and prophecy fulfilled would be performed.

In the next statement, these seventy heptades are broken
up as follows: "Know and understand: From the going
forth of a decree for restoring and rebuilding Jerusalem
unto Messiah the Prince are seven sevens, and sixty-and-
two sevens; the streets shall be restored, and built again;
it is decided and shall be, though in distress of times."
The point from which these periods of seven are reckoned
is the date of a commandment to restore and rebuild Jerusalem. But what commandment is thus referred to? It
cannot be the edict of Cyrus,[*] or its repetition by Darius
Hystaspis;[†] for these had respect only to the Temple, and
said nothing whatever about the city. There remain, however, only two edicts to one or other of which it can be assigned. These are the commission to Ezra in the seventh
year of Artaxerxes Longimanus;[‡] and the letter to Asaph, the
chief forester, given in Nehemiah,[§] in the twentieth year of
the same monarch. It is true, indeed, that the commission to
Ezra does not name the city, but it implies the existence of
a place which he was to bring under civic government; and
so this may very well be taken as the starting-point for these

---

[*] Ezra i., 1-4; vi., 3-5.
[‡] Ibid. vii., 12-26.
[†] Ibid. vi., 1-12.
[§] Neh. ii., 8.

seventy heptades. Now, if this be so, forty-nine years are
allowed for the settlement of affairs at Jerusalem; and of
these we can account for thirteen under Ezra and twelve
under Nehemiah, making together twenty-five. But after
an absence of nine years, Nehemiah returned to Jerusalem
toward the end of the reign of Longimanus, and this brings
the total up to thirty-four.* It is, moreover, probable that
he lived for fifteen years more, for he mentions Joiada as
high-priest;† and his father Eliashib is said to have died
in the eleventh year of Darius Nothus. Now, the eleventh
year of Darius Nothus was forty-five years from the seventh of Artaxerxes, and so there are only four years to be
accounted for.‡ That the city was built and fortified in
"troublous times" is abundantly evident from the record
left by Nehemiah himself. So far, therefore, there is a very
close approximation between the prediction and the history.

The next portion of the prophecy relates to the interval
between the reorganization of the city under Nehemiah and
the appearance of the Messiah. We continue to give it in
Dr. Cowles's version: "And after sixty-two sevens, Messiah
shall be cut off, and there shall be nothing more to him.§
Then the people of a prince that shall come shall destroy
the city and the sanctuary; its end shall be with that sweep-
ing flood; even unto the end of the war desolations are determined. One seven shall make the covenant effective to

---

* See Alexander's "Kitto's Cyclopedia," vol. iii., p. 307.

† Neh. xiii., 28.

‡ Pusey's "Lectures on Daniel the Prophet," p. 174.

§ The translation in our version, "but not for himself," makes the
words mean that Messiah died for the sins of others, and not for his
own. This is a truth, but it is not the truth taught here. The words
imply "there is nothing more to him with them." The people reject
him, and he rejects them. We cannot, therefore, quote this as a proof
text for vicarious atonement, though that doctrine is implied in some of
the other clauses of this passage.

many. The middle of the seven shall make sacrifice and offerings cease : then down upon the summit of the abomination comes the desolator, even till a complete destruction, determined, shall be poured upon the desolate." Here it will be convenient to go back to the date of the edict of Artaxerxes, in the seventh year of his reign. That, according to Pusey, corresponds with 457 B.C. So, calculating sixty-nine sevens, or four hundred and eighty-three years from that date, we come to the year 26 A.D. But it is well known by those acquainted with chronology that Christ was born four years earlier than the first of the era which we call by his name. Therefore, at the year 26 A.D., our Lord would be really thirty years of age ; and we know[*] that his baptism, or public manifestation to the people, took place when he began to be about thirty years of age.

Further, at the end of half a seven of years, or in the middle of the heptade, Messiah, according to this prediction, was to cause the sacrifice and offerings to cease. Now, if we suppose this to refer to the fact that Christ's death, being a real and proper sacrifice for sin, virtually abolished all those under the law, which were only typical, we have here a date harmonizing with that of the Crucifixion. It is as near as possible demonstrable from the Gospel by John that our Saviour's public ministry lasted three years and a half ;[†] and this is corroborated by the parable of the barren fig-tree,[‡] which seems to indicate that three years of special privilege for the Jews had run their course, and that a fourth, or a portion of a fourth, was to be given to them. Here again, therefore, we have a coincidence of date between the prediction and the history. The Messiah was cut off in the midst of the heptade.

---

* Luke iii., 23.
† See Robinson's "Harmony of the Gospels," Appendix, p. 199.
‡ Luke xiii., 6–9.

Still again it is said, "One seven shall make the covenant effective to many." During the first half of this period, as we have seen, our Lord's personal ministry continued. He was then and thereby confirming the covenant to as many as received him. But the people as a whole would not receive him: "there was nothing to him;" and the remaining three and a half years probably mark the time during which the Gospel was preached to the Jews after Christ's resurrection, before the conversion of the Gentiles showed that the special privileges of the Jews were at an end.

Finally, we have here a very distinct indication of the overthrow of Jerusalem by the Romans. This follows upon the rejection of the Messiah by the people of his own nation, and is connected with it here; not because it was to come immediately after it in time, but because it was to be a part, at least, of the punishment of those national sins which culminated in the crucifixion of the Lord of Glory. "The connection," says Pusey,* "is not of time, but of cause and effect. Some forty years were allowed in which individuals might save themselves from that untoward generation. But the doom of the whole was fixed. They had pronounced upon themselves their sentence, "*We have no King but Cæsar.*" Our Lord, in that tender mourning over Jerusalem, pronounced that its day was past. "If thou hadst known, even thou, at least in this thy day, the things which belong unto thy peace! but now they are hid from thine eyes. For the days shall come upon thee, that thine enemies shall cast a trench about thee, and compass thee round, and keep thee in on every side, and shall lay thee even with the ground, and thy children within thee; and they shall not leave in thee one stone upon another; be-

---

* "Lectures on Daniel the Prophet," p. 188.

cause thou knewest not the time of thy visitation."* Thus
has the Saviour amplified in his prediction what Daniel has
here outlined, and every reader of Josephus knows how fully
and how fatally both prophecies were verified.

The exposition which we have given of this section of
Daniel's predictions, and of the manner of its fulfilment, is
fitted to stir the heart even of the most indifferent. For
myself, I feel awed by the sense of the nearness of God,
which comes over me when I read these verses, and remember how they have been confirmed by the events of which
Calvary was the scene.† God is in this history of a truth.
But let us not forget that it differs from ordinary history
only in the fact that here we are permitted to read out of
the book of the divine purpose and prescience ; while in
other cases that record is hidden from our eyes. GOD IS IN
ALL HISTORY as really, and as much, as he was in this. How
solemn, yet how reassuring also, is the thought! "The
Lord reigneth! let the earth rejoice, and the multitude of
the isles be glad thereof."

BUT GOD IS IN THIS BOOK as really as he is in history.
Here is an arch spanning the gulf of half a millennium.
Who built it? Such a structure it is beyond the skill of
human architecture to plan, and the might of human engi-
neering to construct. You cannot account for its existence
without admitting that it is the production of God. We can
clearly trace this portion of Daniel to a date long before the

---

* Luke xix., 42–44.

† This fulfilment is in no degree less marvellous, even if we accept
(which we are by no means disposed to do) the era of the Maccabees as
the date of the Book of Daniel. There is no evading the force of this
prophecy in that way ; for we have evidence of the existence of this
prediction when the Greek version of the Old Testament was made, and
that is quite enough to prove that it could not have been a human in-
vention.

birth of Christ. It was a well-known prophecy among the Jews, and they began to cavil at its genuineness and authenticity only when they found that, fairly interpreted, it pointed to Jesus of Nazareth as the promised Messiah. Its structure is not such as a pretender to prescience would be likely to adopt; for there is nothing so perilous for a false prophet as to attempt in any way to fix the date of the event which he affects to foretell.

Again, the facts by which it was fulfilled were mainly such as could not have been manipulated for the purpose of its accomplishment. The Crucifixion, for example, was an event which could not have been planned beforehand by impostors who wanted to make it appear that they were fulfilling a prophecy; yet by it, in a wonderful way — unthought of even by Christ's own followers at the time — the sacrifices and offerings were made to cease. We must say, therefore, of this prediction, as the magicians said to Moses when their enchantments were at fault, "This is the finger of God!"

But this prophecy does not stand alone. It is one of a series, the members of which are indissolubly connected, and must stand or fall together. Thus it gives support to the whole revelation of which it forms a part; and is itself a supernatural fact which laughs to scorn all the arguments of that sceptical philosophy which presumes to say that the supernatural is impossible. No hypothesis can stand before a certainly established fact that contradicts it. Here, then, in the fact of this prediction, known and acknowledged as in existence for at least two hundred years before the events by which it was fulfilled, we have something superhuman. No sagacious forethought, no shrewdness in guessing at what is in the future, will explain this. It is either inexplicable, or it is divine; and we need not adopt the alternative that it is inexplicable when the other fully fits into and explains all the facts of the case. I am the more particu-

lar to insist on this, because, in recent controversies about
the possibility of miracles, I do not think that enough has
been made by Christian apologists of the fact of prophecy.
What need is there to argue an *à priori* question in the
presence of a fact? Let our sceptical apostles of "modern
thought" explain on natural principles such facts as the existence of this prophecy and its fulfilment, and it will be
something to the purpose. Is not the great principle of the
inductive philosophy something to this effect—"that nothing which claims to rest on actual fact is to be rejected on
examination?" And is it not an axiom in science "that
nothing shall be accepted as a cause which is not adequate
to produce the effect that is attributed to it?" Let these
principles be applied to the facts brought out to-night, and
I think that every candid inquirer will be led to the admission that God is here of a truth.

Finally, we may see in this prophecy, written as with a
sunbeam, this other truth, that GOD IS IN CHRIST. The lines
of prophecy coming from many quarters, and given at different times, all converge toward and meet in Jesus of Nazareth, designating him as both Lord and Christ. The well-
known words of Micah point out his birthplace; many utterances made to David, and through him, indicate his parentage; the marvellous oracle of Isaiah regarding "the Servant of the Lord" details the manner of his life, and the character of his death; and here in the prediction of the seventy
heptades, dates, the most crucial of tests, are given. Now
all these fit precisely into his history, even as in an old-fash-
ioned indenture, the edges of the upper portion correspond
in every minute particular to those of the lower. Were
there no other predictions than these, they would be enough
to mark him out as the Great Deliverer. But when we
have, in addition, a multitude of others, all fulfilled in him,
why should we hesitate for a moment about receiving him?

Be sure that, in believing on Jesus, you are following no cunningly devised fable; but are becoming the disciples of him to whom God has pointed, by the finger of Moses and David, and Isaiah and Jeremiah, and Micah and Daniel, as well as by that of John the Baptist, saying, "Behold the Lamb of God, which taketh away the sin of the world!" In building on this foundation, you are not laying stones on a quicksand, in which they disappear as soon as you have placed them, but you are resting them on the immovable Rock of Ages. In venturing on this bridge, you are not trusting yourself to a tiny plank which will break beneath your weight, but you are treading on a structure stable as the throne of God itself. "God is in Christ, reconciling the world unto himself; not imputing their trespasses unto them." Salvation comes through confidence in him, and loyalty to him. But remember that it is death to reject him. He who spared not the people of his choice, and the city of his habitation, but delivered them up to destruction for their unbelief, will not spare you. Thus alike the goodness and the severity of God call upon us anew to-night to repent and return to him: his goodness in sending the Messiah to take away sin by the sacrifice of himself; and his severity in punishing the Jews for their neglect of the great salvation. Let not the call be unheeded by us. Rarely have I felt the strength of the foundation on which, as a minister of the Gospel, I stand, as I do at this moment. If Christ is not certainly the Son of God, then there is no certainty. If this is not proof that he is the author of everlasting salvation to all them that obey him, then all proof is impossible. I repeat, therefore, with a firmer emphasis, and a stronger assurance than ever, the precious words, "This is a faithful saying, and worthy of all acceptation, that Christ Jesus came into the world to save sinners." But as I think of old Jerusalem, and see the Roman eagle shining in the lurid light of the conflagration that is consuming the Temple on Moriah, I am constrained to add, " Because of unbelief, they were broken off ; and thou standest by faith. Be not high-minded, but fear ; for if God spared not the natural branches, take heed lest he also spare not thee."

XI.

THE VISION ON THE BANKS OF THE HID-DEKEL.

DANIEL x., xi.

THE law of gradual development seems to pervade the government of God, and may be traced alike in the material and spiritual departments of his administration. The earth was not called into existence precisely as it now is, but was prepared by a long series of progressive changes for the abode of the human race. The stalk of ripened grain does not spring up in a moment from the corn of wheat planted in the soil, but there is first the blade, then the ear, and then the full corn in the ear. The tidal wave does not sweep in upon the shore all at once; but it flows in steadily increasing strength, until its height is reached. The man does not come into the world full-grown, as it was fabled that Minerva sprung from the brain of Jupiter; but he is first an infant, then a child, then a youth, and so from hour to hour he "ripes" into maturity. So the revelation which God has given to men has grown into its completeness. The primal promise to our common parents in paradise was the first faint ray that emanated from the coming Sun of Righteousness; but as the morning of the race wore on, that solitary beam expanded, through the Abrahamic covenant, the Mosaic economy, and the prophetic writings, until at length, foreheralded by the Baptist as the morning-star, the divine luminary arose "with healing under his wings."

But what was thus characteristic of revelation as a whole is equally apparent in the communications made to individual prophets; and just as, to-day, we measure our growth by the increase in our understanding and appreciation of their words, so they themselves attained their altitudes of spiritual perception by degrees, and their loftiest peak was also their last. In none of them all is this more conspicuous than in Daniel. While he was yet a youth he received, in connection with the dream of Nebuchadnezzar, a vision of the four monarchies, and the great spiritual kingdom of the Son of man, by which they were to be destroyed. Definite in its great outstanding features, that prophecy was meagre in details. But in the later visions which were given to the prophet himself, the outline of the royal dream was filled in, at first with some leading events in the history of the world, and latterly with the particular details of a critical period in the experience of the Jewish people. The vision of the four beasts is an amplification of the interpretation of Nebuchadnezzar's dream; while again the account of the conflicts between the ram and the he-goat, with the appendix concerning the little horn, is a supplement to the description of the four beasts; and the prophecy of the seventy heptades gives definiteness to the time of the appearing of him who in the one case is represented as a stone cut out of the mountain without hands, and in the other is spoken of as the Son of man who received a kingdom from the Ancient of Days.

Once more, the vision which Daniel received "by the side of the great river, the Hiddekel," and which is contained in the eleventh chapter, soon to be considered, is an expansion of that described in the eighth chapter into such fulness of incident that it reads almost like a history of the times to which it refers. As the vision of the seventh chapter is to that of the second, so is that of the eleventh to that of the eighth. Thus these prophecies lead us from a general summary of the future as a whole into minute particulars of special chapters in the history of the peculiar people; and by so much the more detailed their statements are, by so much the stronger is the proof which their fulfilment furnishes of the divine origin of the communications which Daniel received. In the drawing of a map, the scholar begins with the outline of the country, and seeks to define its boundaries; then he puts in its physical features of mountain-ranges and rivers; then he marks out its divisions into states and counties; and then he inserts the principal towns. Each new stage in his progress thus increases his liability to err, and is therefore a more searching test of the accuracy and extent of his knowledge than that which went before it. So Daniel, in this wonderful series of predictions, goes on from the general to the particular, and brings in at every step new details by which his accuracy may be tested, and by which, if his writings stand the ordeal which they have themselves prepared, his inspiration may be abundantly established.

The latest of his visions is contained, for the most part, in the eleventh chapter of his book; the tenth being what Auberlen has well styled the prologue, and the twelfth what the same suggestive author has called the epilogue. For the present we must confine our attention to the two former, and even in our consideration of them it will be impossible to give more than the merest outline of their contents, with an indication of their fulfilment in the pages of the secular historians who have described the events to which they refer.

The date of this revelation was the third year of Cyrus, King of Persia. This corresponds with the seventy-third year of Daniel's own captivity; so that if we were correct in our conjecture that he was a boy of fourteen years of age when he was taken to Babylon, he must have been fourscore

and seven years old at the time when this "thing" was revealed to him. This, therefore, is the latest communication
which he gave to his people, and the last glimpse which we
get of himself. He had not set out, probably on account of
his extreme old age, with the exiles who returned to Jerusalem after the issuing of the edict of Cyrus. Perhaps, also,
he felt that he might be of more service to Zerubbabel and
his companions by remaining at the seat of the imperial
government than he could have been by accompanying them
to the Holy City. At least, we do not hear of his having
gone to them; and the testimony of tradition is that he died
in Shushan, where a monument which Benjamin of Tudela
reports that he saw in front of one of the Jewish synagogues was said to have been erected to his memory.

He was at this time by the side of the great river, the
Hiddekel, or Tigris, and gave himself up to earnest prayer
to God, accompanied with marks of humiliation and sorrow.
In his own words, he "was mourning three full weeks, he ate
no pleasant bread, neither came flesh nor wine in his mouth,
neither did he anoint himself at all, till three whole weeks
were fulfilled." Now, a question arises as to the cause of
this grief on the part of the prophet, and we find the probable answer in the fact that unexpected difficulties had
arisen before those who had gone to Jerusalem, so that they
were discouraged and well-nigh hopeless. The state of
matters is described by Ezra* thus: "Now when the adversaries of Judah and Benjamin heard that the children of the
captivity builded the temple unto the Lord God of Israel;
then they came to Zerubbabel, and to the chief of the fathers, and said unto them, Let us build with you: for we
seek your God, as ye do; and we do sacrifice unto him
since the days of Esar-haddon king of Assur, which brought

---

* Ezra iv., 1-5.

us up hither. But Zerubbabel, and Jeshua, and the rest of
the chief of the fathers of Israel, said unto them, Ye have
nothing to do with us to build a house unto our God ; but
we ourselves together will build unto the Lord God of Israel, as king Cyrus the king of Persia hath commanded us.
Then the people of the land weakened the hands of the
people of Judah, and troubled them in building, and hired
counsellors against them, to frustrate their purpose, all the
days of Cyrus king of Persia, even until the reign of Darius
king of Persia." Now, remembering what we said in our
last discourse concerning the interest, not patriotic only, but
pious, which the Jews had in their city and Temple, and the
deep concern which Daniel had for the cause with which the
chosen people were identified, we have no difficulty in believing that the arrival at Shushan of the counsellors hired
by the adversaries to frustrate the purpose of the returned
exiles, was the occasion of that sadness which prompted
Daniel to the fasting which he has so minutely described.

At the end of his three weeks' mourning and supplication,
he was blessed with the vision of " a certain man clothed
in linen, whose loins were girded with fine gold of Uphaz ;
his body also was like the beryl, and his face as the appearance of lightning, and his eyes as lamps of fire, and his arms
and his feet like in color to polished brass, and the voice of
his words like the voice of a multitude." This description,
according as it does in almost every particular with that
given by John of Him who appeared in Patmos, and called
himself "Alpha and Omega, the first and the last,"* leads
us to conclude that the mysterious stranger was none other
than the Son of man, to whom, in Daniel's former vision,
the kingdom had been given by the Ancient of Days, and at
whose girdle John saw the keys of Hades and of Death.

---

* See Rev. i., 10–16.

As in the case of Paul journeying to Damascus, the men who accompanied him heard a voice, but saw no man, though the Lord appeared to him in the way, so this celestial one was visible to Daniel, and not to those who were with him; though it is probable that they heard the sound of one speaking, and that may explain why "a great quaking fell upon them, so that they fled to hide themselves."

Thus the prophet was left alone, looking on the great vision, until "there remained no strength in him," and he sunk into a deep sleep, with his face toward the earth. Out of this unconsciousness he was roused by the voice which was like the voice of a multitude, and the hand of a heavenly one touched him, and lifted him upon his knees and the palms of his hands. Then, as he stood trembling, in spite of the soothing ministrations of the spiritual attendant, he heard these words: "Fear not, Daniel: for from the first day that thou didst set thine heart to understand, and to chasten thyself before thy God, thy words were heard, and I am come for thy words. But the prince of the kingdom of Persia withstood me one-and-twenty days: but, lo, Michael, one of the chief princes, came to help me; and I remained there with the kings of Persia. Now I am come to make thee understand what shall befall thy people in the latter days: for yet the vision is for many days."* This prince of the kingdom of Persia is evidently not a man, but an evil angel, who may be supposed to have received from the Prince of Darkness the special commission to foster the bad influences in the Persian Empire, and, if possible, to thwart and overturn the purpose of God concerning it. In his character and actions, he is the adversary both of the good angel who is here conversing with Daniel, and of Michael, the archangel, who had come to the assistance of his subor-

---

* Dan. x., 12-14.

dinate. We thus learn that among the hosts of God there are gradations in rank and influence, and that angels are put by the Lord in charge of the nations. It would seem also that Satan has employed some of his subtlest and most powerful spiritual agents in working among the governments of earth to counteract and, if possible, to neutralize and overcome, the efforts of the good angels to advance the welfare of the human race and the glory of God.

In other portions of the Word of God we find language employed which warrants the belief that individual saints have their guardian angels ;* and in our last lecture we found one such angel in attendance upon Daniel ; but if we admit that these spiritual beings may influence the affairs of men as units, there is nothing unreasonable in recognizing that their ministry affects also the history and destiny of nations. Accordingly, we find mention in this chapter of a good angel, who had the care of God's people. Over him, and apparently at the head of those who were employed in similar services, was Michael, who is elsewhere called the Archangel,† and who is ready to come with assistance in all moments of emergency. Against these, Satan and his legions wage ceaseless war ; and reference is made here to two of his subordinate agents—the one named the Prince of Persia, because his mission was to thwart all movements tending to the prosperity of the Jews in that empire ; and the other styled the Prince of Grecia,‡ because, with the same object in view, his attention was confined to the realm of Greece. It was natural, therefore, that the good angel, who might be regarded as the guardian of his nation, should be sent to Daniel at this time to give him this revelation. He had just been engaged in the very matters affecting the interests of

---

* Matt. xviii., 10.   † Dan. xii., 1 ; Jude 9 ; Rev. xii., 7.
‡ Dan. x., 20.

those who had gone back to Jerusalem which had furnished
the occasion of Daniel's special humiliation and prayer;
and the words which he drops, as it were, incidentally, in
explanation of the tardiness of his appearance, give to the
venerable man of God the assurance that, though for a season evil counsels would prevail with the Persian monarch,
to the delay of the work which had been commenced in the
Holy City, yet ultimately the interests of the returned exiles
would be cared for, and their desires fulfilled. As Auberlen says, " He lets the prophet catch a glimpse of the invisible struggles between the princes of the angels, in which it
is decided who is to exert the determining influence on the
worldly monarch : whether the God-opposing spirit of the
world, or the good spirit whose aim it is to further the interests of God's kingdom. We are wont to speak in a spir-
itualizing way of a struggle between the good and the evil
spirit in man, and Holy Scripture teaches us to regard such
a struggle as real and substantial. But the angelic influences, of which we have more particular knowledge through
the language of Jesus and his apostles, are not essentially
different from this. The liberty of human actions is not
hereby taken away, for the spirits exercise no compelling
influence on men's hearts, and their chief activity consists
probably in the arrangement of outward events. The question about the relation of the Divine government to human
liberty rather loses, than gains, in difficulty, when we take
the element of angelic ministry into consideration."*

The reception of such information concerning the immediate future of his people, together with the intimation of
the fact that he was about to be informed of what should

---

* "Daniel and the Revelation," by Carl August Auberlen, translated
by Rev. A. Saphir, p. 57. See, also, "Excursus on the Angelology of
Daniel," in "Speaker's Commentary," vi., pp. 348–351.

befall them in the latter days, completely unmanned the venerable prophet, so that he set his face toward the ground, and became dumb. But one "like the similitude of the sons of men touched his lips," and the first use he made of his recovered power of utterance was to say, "O my lord, by the vision my sorrows are turned upon me, and I have retained no strength. For how can the servant of this my lord talk with this my lord? for as for me, straightway there remained no strength in me, neither is there breath left in me."* This brought new words of comfort from the angel, whereby Daniel was strengthened. Then, resuming his former theme, the heavenly revealer indicated that he had to return to fight again with the Persian evil angel, and that while he was going forth for, or continuing, that conflict, the prince of Grecia would come, and a new battle would begin with him, in which the representative of God's people would be left to his own resources, with the single exception of the assistance of Michael.

This description of the conflicts in the spirit-world between the rival angels foreshadows the opposition encountered by Zerubbabel, Ezra, Nehemiah, and their compatriots during the reigns of the Persian kings Darius Hystaspis, Xerxes, and Artaxerxes, and also that which, at a later time, the descendants of the restorers of Jerusalem met with at the hands of the Syrian representatives of the Greek Empire. It prepares the way, therefore, for the literal statements which follow in the eleventh chapter,† and from which we learn that, while the Persian kingdom lasted, the enmity of the world-power to the people of God would be largely restrained, and the monarchs would be either posi-

---

* Dan. x., 16, 17.

† The divisions into chapters here are singularly unfortunate, and ought to be disregarded by the English reader. The tenth, eleventh, and twelfth chapters should be read in continuous connection.

tively favorable to them, or, at least, indisposed to harm
them. But with the Grecian Empire, especially in one of
the four divisions into which it was to be broken up, a different course would be pursued, and the descendants of Israel would be reduced by it for a season to the most terrible extremities.

The revelation is introduced with the remarkable phrase,
" I will show you that which is written in the Scriptures of
truth," which, of course, refers not to the book which we
call the Bible, but to that of the divine foreknowledge and
purposes ; and the prophet, as a man greatly beloved, is
permitted, through the eye of the angel, to read so much of
that as God chose to communicate to him. Thus, all history is already written in the plan and prescience of Deity.
If its events were not certain, they could not be thus fore-
known. Yet that they are certain does not interfere with
the liberty of those by whose agency they are brought about.
This looks like a logical impossibility. But let us remember that we are speaking of God, and then we shall begin to
see that infinity cannot be compressed into a finite syllogism.
That we cannot understand how these two propositions can
be both true, may be admitted ; but it does not follow that
they are absolutely inconsistent with each other, in the administration of God. At least, we must be ourselves infinite
before we can determine ; and, even as we are, I do not see
how any man, looking even at the course of his own life, can
get quit, on the one hand, of the overruling control of God,
or, on the other, of the freedom of his own will. There are,
and always will be, the two sides of this subject, and our
wisdom is to accept them both. He who runs off in the direction of the absolutism of God will end in fatalism. He
who accepts only the freedom of man will land himself at
length in chance. But the disciple of Christ accepts them
both ; and, adoring where he cannot comprehend, exclaims,

with Paul, "O the depth of the riches both of the wisdom
and knowledge of God! how unsearchable are his judg-
ments, and his ways past finding out! For who hath known
the mind of the Lord? or who hath been his counsellor?
Or who hath first given to him, and it shall be recompensed
unto him again? For of him, and through him, and to him,
are all things: to whom be glory forever. Amen."*

The prophecy contained in the eleventh chapter may
be divided into three parts, increasing in circumstantiality
as they advance. There is, first, a brief description of the
Persian and Grecian empires; second, a sketch of the more
important events in the struggles between the kings of Syria
and Egypt; and, third, a detailed and minute account of the
character and actions of Antiochus Epiphanes.

The prediction opens thus: "Behold, there shall stand
up yet three kings in Persia; and the fourth shall be far
richer than they all: and by his strength through his riches
he shall stir up all against the realm of Grecia. And a
mighty king shall stand up, that shall rule with great dominion, and do according to his will. And when he shall stand
up, his kingdom shall be broken, and shall be divided toward the four winds of heaven; and not to his posterity, nor
according to his dominion which he ruled: for his kingdom
shall be plucked up, even for others besides those." The
three kings yet to appear were Cambyses, Smerdis, and
Darius Hystaspis. The fourth was Xerxes, commonly now
identified with the Ahasuerus of the Book of Esther, whose
wealth, and whose immense expedition against Greece,
reckoned by many as consisting of five millions of men, are
well known. He was succeeded by other Persian monarchs,
but no mention is made of them, because they were of no
account in the conflicts between Persia and Greece, and be-

---

* Rom. xi., 33–36.

cause it was in the reign of Xerxes, and by the battle of
Salamis, that the Persian Empire received that blow from
which it never recovered, and from which, therefore, its decay may be dated.   Moreover, it was the invasion of Greece
by Xerxes which was put forth by Alexander as his pretext
for attacking Persia.   Therefore, connecting effect with
cause, the prediction leaps over a hundred and fifty years,
and lets us see the nemesis following the crime even after
three half-centuries; thereby reminding us of the saying,
"God does not pay at the end of every week, but at the
last he pays."

The character and success of Alexander are summed up
in a sentence; and the partition of his empire among his
generals after his death is accurately foreshadowed, according to the account which we have already given in these
pages.*

The second portion of the prophecy, extending from the
fifth to the nineteenth verse, epitomizes the more prominent of the wars between "the king of the north;" that is,
the dynasty of the Seleucidæ, which occupied the throne of
Syria, and "the king of the south," that is, the dynasty of
the Ptolemies, which ruled over Egypt.   These have been
particularized, because Palestine, lying between the two, was
grievously wasted in their long-continued conflict.   As Luther pithily puts it, "The Jews, placed thus between the
door and the hinge, were sorely tormented on both sides.
Now they fell a prey to Egypt, and anon to Syria, as the
one kingdom or the other got the better, and they had to
pay dearly for their neighborhood: specially when that impious man was king in Syria whom histories call Antiochus Epiphanes.   He assaulted the Jews most fiercely, and
raged and slaughtered like a demon among them.   It was

---

* See *ante*, pp. 145–149.

on account of this wretched and cruel villain that the vision was given to comfort the Jews, whom he was to torment with all kinds of plagues."*

The sixth verse thus begins the sketch: "And in the end of years they shall join themselves together; for the king's daughter of the south shall come to the king of the north to make an agreement: but she shall not retain the power of the arm; neither shall he stand, nor his arm: but she shall be given up, and they that brought her, and he that begat her, and he that strengthened her in these times." This describes an attempt to patch up an alliance between the two dynasties when Ptolemy Philadelphus gave his daughter Berenice in marriage to Antiochus Theos, the condition being that he should divorce his wife Laodice, and exclude her children from succession to his throne. But no good came out of the arrangement, for Ptolemy died two years after; and then Antiochus, having put Berenice away, took back his former wife Laodice, who, fearing her husband's fickleness, procured his murder, and subsequently, through her son, caused the death of Berenice with her son and servants.

Then follows, in the seventh, eighth, and ninth verses, an account of an expedition undertaken by the brother of Berenice, here called "one out of a branch of her roots," and known in history as Ptolemy Euergetes, who sought, by an invasion of Syria, to avenge her murder. In this he was so far successful that he made himself master of all the country as far east as the Tigris, and returned to Egypt with forty thousand talents of silver, a vast number of golden vessels, and two thousand five hundred images, among

---

* Quoted by Auberlen, in "Daniel and the Revelation," p. 59. See an admirable summary of the history of the Jews during this period in the "Speaker's Commentary," vol. vi., p. 377.

which were many of the Egyptian idols, which Cambyses, on his conquest of Egypt, three hundred years before, had removed to Persia.*   He outlived Seleucus four years, and thus "continued more years than the king of the north."

The next section of the chapter refers to Antiochus the Great, and his struggles with the kings of Egypt during his reign.   This king, at first the ally, and after two years the successor, of his brother Seleucus Ceraunus, prosecuted the hereditary quarrel with Egypt vigorously, and, in the beginning, with success.   Afterward, however, he was defeated with great loss, and compelled to enter into a peace with his rival, which lasted for fourteen years.   This is clearly foreshadowed in the words, "the king of the south shall be moved with choler, and shall come forth and fight with him, even with the king of the north: and he shall set forth a great multitude; but the multitude shall be given into his hand."   But the Egyptian monarch could not follow up his advantage, for "his heart was lifted up;" and though he "cast down many ten thousands," yet he was not strengthened thereby.   Accordingly, at the end of fourteen years, when Egypt had a boy of five years old for king, Antiochus renewed the war, "setting forth a greater multitude than the former."   On this occasion he was assisted by many Jews, who are here called violent men (for so the word rendered "robbers" may be understood) "of thy people."   In acknowledgment of their services, Antiochus granted many privileges and favors to the Jews, and it might appear, at first sight, that they had made a valuable alliance in securing the friendship of the Syrian monarch; but, in reality, they made a great mistake.   The true policy of the Jews was to stand aloof from both parties; but in seeking to gain

---

* See Prideaux, "Connection of the Old and New Testaments," etc., vol. ii., p. 76.

protection from Antiochus, they very speedily found that they had gone for refuge into a lion's den. Their expectations, though at the time apparently realized, were in the end disappointed; for as Keil has said, "The apostasy of one party among the Jews from the law of their fathers, and their adoption of heathen customs, contributed to bring about that oppression with which the theocracy was visited by Antiochus Epiphanes."[*]

During this campaign, Antiochus the Great, after an engagement at the source of the Jordan, took Tyre and Sidon, and was received by the Jews in their metropolis with great gladness, and entertained by them with the most liberal hospitality. So "he stood in the glorious land;" but his visit was more a calamity than an honor, for the garrison left in the castle by the Egyptian general proved so obstinate that he was compelled to bring up his whole army to reduce it, and during the siege the country was eaten up by the soldiers. The city, too, suffered such damage that it was nearly ruined; and so it came to pass as it is here written, "he shall stand in the glorious land, which by his hand shall be consumed."[†]

In his desire to possess Egypt as well as Syria, Antiochus gave his daughter Cleopatra in marriage to Ptolemy Epiphanes; but his plan was frustrated by the fact that she sided with her husband rather than her father, according to the statement made in this prophecy, "He shall give him

---

[*] Quoted by Dr. Strong, in Lange, vol. xiii., Old Testament, p. 244.

[†] This is the explanation given by Prideaux in his "Connection of the Old and New Testaments," etc., vol. ii., p. 134; but a different interpretation is offered in the "Speaker's Commentary," which renders the phrase "consumption shall be in his hand," and, rejecting the application of the words to the exhaustion of the land consequent upon the siege referred to in the text, leaves the difficulty thereby created among those which are as yet unsolved.

the daughter of women, corrupting her: but she shall not stand on his side, neither be for him." When he could not succeed against Egypt, he turned his arms against the islands of the Ægean, and, after various successes, he entered on a war with the Romans, in which he was defeated by Scipio, who assumed the name of Asiaticus, in honor of his victory. Compelled to give up all his possessions west of Mount Taurus and to pay the whole expenses of the war, Antiochus subjected his kingdom to immense taxation; and in an attempt to rob the temple of Elymais, he was slain by the infuriated people. Thus were fulfilled the words of this prophecy: "After this shall he turn his face unto the isles, and shall take many: but a prince for his own behalf shall cause the reproach offered by him to cease; without his own reproach he shall cause it to turn upon him. Then he shall turn his face toward the fort of his own land: but he shall stumble and fall, and not be found."

He was succeeded by his son Seleucus Philopator, who was bound by the agreement of Antiochus to pay a thousand talents annually as tribute to the Romans; and who, to raise that sum, became, according to the expression of the twentieth verse here, "a sender of taxgatherers over the glory of the kingdom." During the absence of both his sons, he was poisoned by Heliodorus, his treasurer, whose ambition it was to mount the throne in his room. We have thus the verification of the twentieth verse: "Then shall stand up in his estate a raiser of taxes in the glory of the kingdom: but within few days" (he reigned only eleven years) "he shall be destroyed, neither in anger nor in battle."

From this point on to the close of the eleventh chapter, we have an account of the character and cruelties of Antiochus Epiphanes, concerning whom, in a former discourse, we have so fully spoken.* How he should come to the

---

* See *ante*, pp. 152, 157.

kingdom, not by right of inheritance (for the eldest son of
his deceased brother was still alive), but by flatteries ;* how,
after various military successes, he should depose the Jewish high-priest, Onias III., from his office ;† how, after
making a covenant with his Egyptian rival, he should deal
deceitfully, and with a small force of his own, but assisted
by Judah, become strong in Edom, Ammon, and Moab ;‡
how he should possess himself of Cœlesyria and Palestine,
and, contrary to the custom of his ancestors, should scatter
liberal largesses among the people of the subject lands, pursuing bribery as a policy,§ is all minutely described in these
verses.

With the same accurate forecast we have here presented
to us the details of his wars with the Egyptians. With great
force on both sides, it was a contest of deceiver with deceiver, but victory belonged to Antiochus ;‖ and it was when
his heart was lifted up by reason of this success that he entered upon those efforts against the Holy Covenant which
have made his name detestable in the estimation alike of
Jews and Christians.¶ 'But as I have already referred to
these matters in detail, I need not dwell upon them here.
Let me only point out that in this remarkable prophecy we
are told, three hundred years before the time, that he should
pollute the Temple of Jerusalem,** and take away the daily
sacrifice ; that he should corrupt some of the chosen people
by his flatteries, and stir up others of them to be strong and
do exploits ;†† that he should exalt himself above every God,
and speak marvellous things against the God of gods, persecuting every faithful Israelite without regard to age or
sex ;‡ that he should honor a false deity with gold and sil-

---

ver and precious stones ;* and that he should make an expedition, first into Armenia, and thence into the East, where
he should come to his end, and none should help him.
Now, all these things actually came to pass. It would, I
fear, exhaust your patience if I were to attempt to show you
here how each verse in the prediction has been fulfilled.
Instead, therefore, of reproducing the history which is thus
so remarkably forewritten, I would recommend you to study
with attention the statements made by the commentators in
their exposition of this chapter ; and though it is the fashion among those who would be accounted scholarly to decry
the writings of Matthew Henry and Albert Barnes, I am
free to confess that, after an amount of reading on this subject which I should not care to repeat, I have found no expositors more clear, more connected, or more judicious than
the two whom I have named.† They are, besides, easily

---

* Verse 38. "The King's own special deity was not of his Grecian
ancestry, but one borrowed from Rome—whether the war-god Mars, father of the Roman people, or Jupiter of the Capitoline Rock, to whom
he began to build a splendid temple at Antioch—in either case, filling
even the Jews, to whom all these divinities might have been thought
equally repugnant, with a new thrill of sorrow, as indicating a disrespect
even of the religion of his own race, and introducing a strange and terrible name." So Stanley expands this verse, " Jewish Church," vol. iii.,
pp. 329, 330.

† The earlier volumes of Mr. Barnes—those, namely, on the Gospels
and the Acts—are meagre enough ; but he improved as he advanced,
and his latest efforts are his best. His commentaries on Job, Daniel,
and the Psalms are every way admirable, and cannot be consulted without advantage. To those writers named above we ought to add the un-
pretending but valuable volume of Dr. Cowles, of Oberlin, and the anno-
tations of Mr. Fuller in the " Speaker's Commentary," although the latter
are in some places halting and unsatisfactory. Dean Stanley, in his last
volume on the Jewish Church, is, as usual, brilliant in description, but he
is too much under the spell of Ewald throughout ; and nowhere more
than in this volume does he verify the criticism of Dr. Pusey, given in

accessible to every one who wishes to study the Word of God, and every reader of their comments will be constrained to come to the conclusion indicated by F. W. Newman in his article on Antiochus Epiphanes in Kitto's "Cyclopædia," that "either this chapter was written after the events, or it was given by inspiration of God." The latter, I fear, is the alternative which that writer would adopt; but the very obscurities which remain in the chapter, despite all the efforts of interpreters to explain them, are inconsistent with that hypothesis, for one writing after the facts had occurred would not have left any such difficulties. Besides, even the Maccabean date of this book does not eliminate the supernatural from its pages, for, as we have seen, the prophecy of the seventy heptades is as clearly beyond the limit of human ingenuity when we regard it as given two hundred as when we estimate it as written five hundred years before its fulfilment. Indeed, even in the estimation of such a critic as Ewald, this book furnished the inspiration by which the handful of Jewish patriots under Judas Maccabæus were moved to the performance of those prodigies of valor by which their Temple was recovered and their religion preserved. But if that be admitted, it is every way more natural to view it as handed down from the exile than to suppose, as he does, that it "sprung from the necessities of the noblest impulses of the age," and "rendered to that age the

---

these words : "It seems to be a principle with Dean Stanley to hold that to be uncertain which is assailed. Conviction amidst contradictions of truth seems to him undue dogmatism. His mind has been remarkably characterized as one which, 'having a poetical faculty of seeing resemblances, lacks the philosophical power of seeing differences.'"—*Preface to Daniel the Prophet*, pp. 26, 27.

All the writers on this chapter from Prideaux downward draw their materials mainly from Josephus and the books of the Maccabees. Milman's "History of the Jews" will be read with interest by young and old alike.

purest service."* The examples of Daniel in the den and the three youths in the furnace quickened the faith of those who were called to suffer for conscience' sake, while the details of this prediction assured them that after a little while their oppressor would be taken away.

It remains that I should look for a moment at the opinion of those who believe that we have in this prediction a reference to the Antichrist of the New Testament as well as to Antiochus. Of these, there are some who think that up to a certain point the description is applicable solely to the Syrian despot, but that from that point he is dropped, and the rest is to be explained of the evil principle or power of which both Paul and John have spoken. But for such an idea we can find no sure foundation. There is nothing in the chapter to indicate that a transition from one subject to another is made ; and if we begin to expound it as referring to the sufferings of the Jews in the conflicts between Syria and Egypt, we must adhere to that principle of interpretation throughout. Others, however, affirm that the Antiochus of this prophecy, though himself an historical personage, in whom all that is here written was accomplished, is also a type of the papal Antichrist, in whom, in a yet more terrible sense, it will be again fulfilled. But it is a question not yet settled, whether the Papacy really is the Antichrist of the New Testament ; and, however that may be solved, it is a perilous thing to make any person in the Old Testament a type, in any proper sense of that word, unless we have authority for doing so in the New Testament itself. No doubt the language here used concerning Antiochus is very similar to that employed by Paul to describe the evil power that is to exalt himself above all that is called God, or that is worshipped ; yet mere resemblance is

---

* Quoted in Stanley's " History of the Jewish Church," vol. iii., p. 336.

not sufficient to warrant the conclusion that we are to look for a minute fulfilment of this prediction in some wicked ruler during the Gospel dispensation. I deem it safer, more reverent, and more instructive also, to see in this chapter a forecast of one great crisis in the history of ancient Israel, and to draw from that the inference that every power, whether temporal or spiritual, which sets itself up against the cause of God, however for a time it may seem to be successful, shall come to an end, and none shall help it. We have thus repeated to us the old truth, which sounds with more than earthly music in the jubilant strophes of the Forty-sixth Psalm, and we hear again the words of Isaiah: "No weapon that is formed against thee shall prosper; and every tongue that shall rise against thee in judgment thou shalt condemn. This is the heritage of the servants of the Lord, and their righteousness is of me, saith the Lord."*

Reverting, now, in conclusion, to the benefit which we may ourselves derive from the study of this portion of Scripture, we may learn, for one thing, that God prepares his people for special trial by special grace. If it be true, as it surely is, that the Lord never gives faith without in some way, ere long, putting it to the test, it is no less so that he never sends tribulation without giving us something to support us under it. He anticipates the evil with his help. His assistance is ever beforehand with our emergency, and in his words of prophecy and promise he has already provided us with all we need in any hour of trial. "He sendeth no man a warfare on his own charges;" and before he sets one out upon a pilgrimage, he puts a staff in his hand to support him by the way. That was the great purpose for which this prediction was given, and the "exploits" which were done by the faithful few who knew their God, and had

---

* Isa. liv., 17.

understanding to recognize the meaning of the revelation which he had given to Daniel, were the outcome of his goodness.

But the relation of this portion of God's Word to the circumstances of the people under Antiochus is precisely that of all his promises to our trials, temptations, and necessities. Every promise of God is a prophecy; and if, knowing him who gives them, we grasp his assurances as firmly as the Maccabeans did in their time of peril, we too shall be valiant for the Lord God of Israel. There is not one among us of any maturity in Christian experience who cannot point to some portion of Scripture that has been to him, in an hour of conflict, or agony, or need, just what this portion of Daniel was to those who "resisted unto blood striving" against the persecuting King of Syria.

One of the most profitable conference-meetings which we ever attended had for its subject "favorite texts." It soon appeared that special interest was felt in the topic by all present, and more than the usual number were eager to make themselves heard, not because they wanted to show themselves, but because they wished a word to be said about the passage which was to them so dear. It came out, also, that every text that was referred to was dwelt upon, not for its literary beauty, but because of a certain experience through which the individual had passed, and in which it had been to him like the hand of God himself, held down for him to grasp. In some cases the verse particularized had been the instrument of conversion, and then were related the circumstances in connection with which the soul had passed from darkness unto light. In others, the words had been the stay of the heart in agony and trial; and then the story of "toiling in rowing" on the midnight lake, and against the howling wind, was rehearsed, while the voice quivered as the speaker referred to the calm influence of the Saviour's " Peace, be still !" Young and old and middle-aged had some special text to honor ; and, as we listened, we all felt that we had never looked so deeply into each other's hearts, or seen so much of the manifold adaptation of the Scripture to the conditions of men, as we did then.

Brethren, there is nothing that can support the soul like the Word of God ; and it would be well for us, in our days of health and happiness, to study its pages so that, when trouble is upon us, we may be able at once to lay hold of the promise which our father has put in it beforehand for our solace and succor. Thus out of each new trial we shall come with a new text, brightened and glorified for us by the experience which it recalls ; and so we shall understand how it happens that, though the words are the same in every copy, the Bible is not the same to every believer ; for, as the years roll on, each writes his autobiography over its verses, and sees something in it which is invisible to all but himself. Oh, if we had but understanding to use its revelations thus, no mousing rationalism would be allowed by us to eat away its treasures, and the deeds of the Maccabeans would be outshone by our steadfast and unflinching adherence to its Lord.

But we may learn, in the second place, from this section of prophecy that faith in the invisible is essential to our getting the full benefit of Scripture. Much may be gained from it in history and in morals, even if we should repudiate everything that is supernatural in its pages. I do not stay now to ask whether this can be done consistently or not. I simply admit that it is possible ; but to obtain the utmost benefit from its words, we must accept its revelation of that which is hidden from mortal sight. The relation of the tenth chapter of Daniel, with its details about the angelic world, to the eleventh, with its descriptions of earthly conflicts, is that of the unseen to the future. So, when the Maccabeans saw the events which Daniel had foretold happening before their eyes, they would have recalled to them the revelation of the invisible by which the prophecy was accompanied, and would be encouraged and supported by the thought that "the angel of the Lord encampeth round about them that fear him, and delivereth them." They would feel that the God of Michael was on their side, and that would nerve them to new courage.

But the revelation of Christ to the eye of the protomartyr stands for us in the same relation to that precious assurance of his, "Lo! I am with you alway, even unto the end of the world;" and if, when we are beleaguered by spiritual enemies, we could but recall the description, "He, being full of the Holy Ghost, looked steadfastly up into heaven, and saw the glory of God, and Jesus standing on the right hand of God, and said, Behold, I see the heavens opened, and the Son of man standing on the right hand of God," we should not be moved by

> " Reviling tones,
> Nor sell our hearts to idle moans,"

but continue firm and unfaltering in our allegiance to our Lord. The promises of Jesus are not to us like the legacies of one long dead; they are not the words merely of a great philosopher, like the Grecian sage, whom death has severed from all personal contact with our modern life. They are the assurances of a living and present though unseen friend; and, when so accepted, they are full of power. Depend upon it, the precious assurance, "My grace is sufficient for thee, my strength is made perfect in weakness," meant far more to Paul, because of the revelation of the unseen in the third heavens which he had so shortly before received. That gave them reality and present availability, and in these were their comforting influence. Let us, therefore, remember that, behind every pledge which this book contains, there is the living though unseen God, and that "he maketh his angels ministering spirits for them that shall be heirs of salvation." This will uphold us in all time of extremity; and the only issue of our calamities will be "to purge and to make us white, even unto the time of the end." The inspiration of Moses' life came from the fact that "he endured as seeing him who is invisible;" and the Bible will be to us no better than the moral maxims of Antoninus or Epictetus, unless we receive its revelation of the unseen in connection with its forecasts of prophecy and promise. The two must go together; for we have no motive to rest in the one unless we accept the other.

XII.

THE EPILOGUE TO THE VISION.

DANIEL xii.

THIS chapter is not only the epilogue to the vision which we considered in our last lecture, but also the formal conclusion to the Book of Daniel as a whole. It stands in a relation, primary and immediate to the predictions which have just preceded it, and secondary and more remote to all those which are contained in this interesting portion of the Sacred Scriptures. Its interpreters may be divided generally into those who regard its announcements as already fulfilled, and those who, denying their accomplishment in the past, are still looking for it in the future.

Its first clause, "at that time," fixes the reference of all that follows to the period spoken of in the closing verses of the eleventh chapter. If, therefore, we were right in expounding that section of Antiochus Epiphanes, we must take this also as relating to the fearful time when that abominable tyrant persecuted the people and defiled the house of Jehovah. It is no objection to this view that this era is described as "a time of trouble such as never was since there was a nation even to that same time;" for, not to say that this expression must be more or less hyperbolical, we have only to read the books of the Maccabees to be convinced that the atrocities committed by Antiochus and his subordinates were such as might well enough be characterized by these emphatic words. Since the days of Daniel, history has recorded many cruelties to which men have been subjected for their faith, both in ancient and modern times; but though those inflicted by Antiochus have been sometimes equalled by others, they certainly have never been exceeded. Hence, there is nothing in this language inconsistent with the interpretation of those who would explain it, as we do, of the time when that brutal monster desolated Jerusalem, and desecrated its Temple.

Neither do we find any difficulty arising out of the last clause of the first verse, which says, "at that time thy people shall be delivered, every one that shall be found written in the book." For the phrase "written in the book" simply means "designated by God as to be delivered," or "known by God, and protected by him, as his own." No doubt the words are very similar to those which are employed in the New Testament description of the last judgment; and they might very well be regarded as alluding to the same thing here, provided there were anything in the preceding context that would make such a reference natural. In the absence of that, however, it is every way safer to content ourselves with explaining the words, as descriptive of the deliverance of God's faithful ones in the days of Judas Maccabæus.

A far more serious objection to this exposition seems to arise from the statement made in the second and third verses: "And many of them that sleep in the dust of the earth shall awake, some to everlasting life, and some to shame and everlasting contempt. And they that be wise shall shine as the brightness of the firmament; and they that turn many to righteousness, as the stars for ever and ever." Here there is, unquestionably, a reference to the resurrection of the dead, and the future state of rewards and punishments. It is idle to attempt, with Barnes, to give these words a figurative sense, and make them describe a general uprising of the people against the Syrian despot.

Every one feels instinctively that such an interpretation is far beneath the full significance of the verse, even though it be admitted, as the author referred to does admit, that there is a typical allusion to the resurrection from the dead.   I do not wonder, therefore, that ingenuous minds turn with dissatisfaction from such an explanation.   Nor is it strange to me that almost all those who, as expositors of the Book of Revelation, believe in two literal resurrections, do also regard these words as referring to one of them, and endeavor to make the predictions with which they are connected fit in with their general system of prophetic interpretation.   But as I have not been able to accept their scheme of prophecy, as, indeed, on quite other grounds than those of mere exigesis I have been constrained hitherto to reject it, I must look for some other exposition which will meet the circumstances of the case.

Is there no interpretation, then, which, while regarding these words as referring to the literal resurrection of the dead, will harmonize also with the view which explains the whole passage of the days of Antiochus?   I think there is ; and it is to me an additional recommendation of the explanation which I am about to present, that I find it in the pages of Auberlen, who is himself an adherent of the pre-millennial school.   I ask your close attention while I endeavor to unfold it.   The phrase "they that be wise," in the third verse of this twelfth chapter, corresponds to — is indeed, in the original, identical with—that rendered "they that understand among the people," in the thirty-third verse of the eleventh chapter.   It recurs in the thirty-fifth verse as, "they of understanding."   Again, the "turning of many to righteousness," in the third verse of the twelfth chapter, answers to the "instructing of many," in the thirty-third verse of the eleventh chapter.   Now here we have the key to the explanation of the reference which is made to the resurrection. The coming-forth of the dead from their graves is not introduced as a new fact which was to occur in the immediate line of the incidents which have been so particularly indicated. It is not a new element in this prophecy, and does not belong to it specially and particularly. The words do not imply that a resurrection of those who had fallen in the Maccabean struggle should immediately follow that struggle. Rather the resurrection is mentioned as a great fact which is to come at the close of all human history, and from it both warning and encouragement are drawn appropriate to the emergency of that dreadful time. It is alluded to for the purpose of setting clearly before the men of that generation the solemn truth—true for all generations as for that—that they who remained faithful to the covenant of their God, and strengthened their brethren in the same course, would be ultimately raised to eternal glory; while they who apostatized from the right path would be eternally lost. The design of the apocalyptic angel thus was to stimulate the Jews of the days of Antiochus to fidelity by the consideration of the momentous individual issues that hung upon their conduct. "We have here," says Auberlen, "a parallel to the epistles to the Seven Churches in the Revelation of John, which contain promises for those who overcome, and threats for those who fall away. The sole purpose for which the resurrection is introduced is to show the causal connection between the behavior of the people during the time of their probation and their eternal state; but not the slightest intimation is given as to the chronological relation between the time of distress and that of resurrection."* In proof of this, we may direct attention to the fact that the phrase "at that time," occurring twice in the first verse, does not appear in either the second or

* "Daniel and the Revelation," by Carl August Auberlen, etc., p. 174.

the third.   In these last no note of time is given.   Hitherto the angel has prophesied the development of history,
without adding any remark or exhortation.   Here, however,
he concludes his predictions by adding the strongest possible incitement to faithful perseverance; an incitement which
must have had all the stronger effect, since, though it is occasionally referred to in earlier prophets, the resurrection
had never before been brought forward so distinctly and
powerfully, and especially had never been shown in its connection with retribution.

This view of the passage is rendered still more probable
when we turn to the history of the period referred to, and
learn that the hope of resurrection to eternal life did sustain
the sufferers under the infliction of the most dreadful cruelties.   Thus, in the seventh chapter of the Second Book of
Maccabees, which contains an account of the martyrdom of
seven brothers and their mother, whose tortures are given
as a specimen of those by which the faithful were tried, we
read that the second son, when he was asked whether he
would eat swine's flesh before he should be punished in
every member of his body, made answer, "No;" and being
put to torture, exclaimed, with his latest breath, "Thou like
a fury takest us out of the present life, but the King of the
world shall raise us up, who have died for his laws, unto
everlasting life."   So, also, the fourth brother said, "It is
good, being put to death by men, to look for hope from God
to be raised up again by him; as for thee, thou shalt have
no resurrection to life."   And the mother, who was marvellous above all, exhorted her sons, saying, "Doubtless the
Creator of the world will also give you breath and life
again, as you now regard not your own selves for his laws'
sake."   In the patient heroism, therefore, of those noble
ones who counted not their lives dear unto them, that they
might keep the ordinance of their God, and who upheld

their hearts by faith in the resurrection to eternal life, we see the fruit of this reference to that grand and crowning miracle which is to put the cope-stone on human history.

Fitly, too, does the allusion to the resurrection at the last bring the whole series of predictions to a close, and lead the angel to say, "Shut up the words, and seal the book even unto the time of the end. Many shall run to and fro, and knowledge shall be increased." "The time of the end" is the appointed time for the fulfilment of these predictions, which was to be marked by an increase of knowledge among men, consequent upon the passing of multitudes from place to place. It is indeed a general law, that knowledge grows in proportion as the facilities of travel between different countries are multiplied. Of this there have been many illustrations in the course of human history. We have a very signal one in our own age; and there was another, no less remarkable in its way, in that to which these prophecies refer; for, after the yoke of Antiochus was broken, the Roman power began to spread over the East; and to this era, when communication between the nations became more easy and more frequent, we trace that general diffusion of the Greek language and literature which, in the purpose of God, was destined to prepare the way for the publication of the Gospel in all lands. The age which culminated in the culture and pre-eminence of Alexandria, with its scholarship and philosophy, and in which the translation of the Old Testament into the Greek language was made, was certainly one to which these words are applicable: "Many shall run to and fro, and knowledge shall be increased....."

After the angel had ceased speaking to Daniel, the prophet saw other two messengers from heaven, standing, one on each side of the river Tigris; and, as he looked and listened, he heard one of these ask the glorious One whom he had first beheld, "How long shall it be to the end of these won-

ders?" He received for answer, with a solemn asseveration
of their truth, the following words : " It shall be for a time,
times, and a half ;* and when he shall have accomplished to
scatter the power of the holy people, all these things shall
be finished." That is to say, it shall be for three years and
a half; and when the tyrant shall have done all that he
could to scatter the power of the Jews, the deliverance shall
come. Daniel, however, did not understand the answer, and
repeated the question which the angel had asked, only in a
slightly different form : " O my Lord, what shall be the end
of these things ?" To this the following reply was given :
" Go thy way, Daniel : for the words are closed up and sealed
till the time of the end. Many shall be purified, and made
white, and tried; but the wicked shall do wickedly : and
none of the wicked shall understand ; but the wise shall understand. And from the time that the daily sacrifice shall
be taken away, and the abomination that maketh desolate
set up, there shall be a thousand two hundred and ninety
days. Blessed is he that waiteth, and cometh to the thousand three hundred and five-and-thirty days. But go thou
thy way, till the end be : for thou shalt rest, and stand in
thy lot at the end of the days."

We have already seen that the desolation of the Temple
by Antiochus extended over three years and six months,
which is here styled " a time and times and the dividing
of time ;" but we cannot pass this note of number without
remarking on the singular coincidences presented by its
frequent recurrence both in history and prophecy. The
drought in the days of Elijah lasted three years and six
months. The little horn which appeared on the head of
the fourth beast was to have the saints given into his hands
" until a time and times and the dividing of time." The

---

* Literally, " a time, two times, and a half."

public ministry of the Messiah was to continue for half a week or heptade of years; that is, for three years and a half. His Gospel was to be preached to the Jews after his ascension for another half-heptade before it was proclaimed to the Gentiles. Then, in the Book of Revelation, it is said that the woman shall be nourished in the wilderness "for a time, and times, and half a time,"* and that the Holy City should be trodden under foot forty and two months, which are three and a half years. Now, all these are marvellous coincidences, and point to the existence of some hidden harmony which has not yet been discovered. I might add that three and a half is the half of the number seven, which, found in the week, has been made the symbol of perfection, and as such frequently recurs in the Word of God. The sacred lamp had seven branches; the seventh was the Sabbatic year; and at the end of seven sevens came the year of Jubilee. So, also, the seventy years of the Captivity were made the basis of the seven seventies of years which were to run their course from the time when the edict to rebuild Jerusalem went forth until the appearance of the Messiah upon the earth. I do not know what to make of all this. I frankly acknowledge that it baffles me to find a reason for it. I merely state the fact, and leave you to ponder it for yourselves, that you may learn how much there is not only in prophecy, but also in history, which lies beyond our ken. The two other dates referred to in verses eleventh and twelfth may be thus explained. The profanation of the Temple by Antiochus continued from the month Ijar, of the year 168 B.C., till the restoration of the worship by Judas Maccabæus on the twenty-fifth day of the ninth month, 165 B.C. This, according to the Seleucid era, occupied twelve hundred and ninety days. Forty five days more bring us to

---

* Rev. xii., 14.

the month Shebat, of 164 B.C., in which Antiochus died—so ending for the time the miseries of the people. Thus the thousand three hundred and five-and-thirty days are accounted for.*

If any choose to regard all this as being not only applicable to Antiochus, but also, through him, typical of the New Testament Antichrist, and should take the days in the history of the one for years in the history of the other, I have only to say that I find nothing, either here or in the New Testament, to sanction such a procedure. For me, the interpretation which I have endeavored to give is sufficient. They who go further leave the domain of certainty for that of speculation, and the very number of their conflicting interpretations is a warning to every expositor not to venture beyond his depth into these dark waters. For myself, I am content to stand upon the shore and wait, like him to whom were first addressed these reassuring words, "Go thy way; for thou shalt rest, and stand in thy lot at the end of the days."

But though there may be some difference of opinion as to the interpretation of the prophecies contained in this chapter, there can be no controversy among Christians as to the lessons of comfort and encouragement which God's people in every age may draw from its verses. I name now only the three most prominent. We have, in the first place, the hope of the suffering saint. "Many of them that sleep in the dust of the earth shall awake, some to everlasting life, and some to shame and everlasting contempt." The doctrine of the resurrection of the dead does not come very distinctly out in the earlier portions of the Old Testament. It is alluded to in some of the Psalms, and is referred to with

---

* See "Critical and Experimental Commentary," by Jamieson: Fausset & Brown. Vol. iv., *in loco.*

somewhat more precision in the Book of Isaiah; while the miracles of Elijah and Elisha must have made many minds among the nation familiar with the idea.   But here, for almost the first time, it is broadly asserted, and that in such a way as to connect it with retribution, and make it an encouragement to fidelity under trial.   Under the old covenant, the sanctions of the divine law were mainly temporal. The blessings promised, and the punishments threatened, had reference, for the most part, to the life that now is.   But here we have an approximation to the New Testament way of treating such subjects, and those who are enduring trial are exhorted to look beyond the present, and to rely that, in the future life, there shall be for them a reward as exalted as their sufferings have been severe.   Of the Lord himself it is said that, because he humbled himself to the death of the cross, *therefore* God hath highly exalted him; and they who in his service, and for their adherence to his laws, are oppressed and persecuted in this world, may depend upon it that in the life that is to come they shall rise to everlasting honor.   Not always shall might be triumphant and truth lie torn and bleeding in the streets; not always shall the wicked prosper, and the righteous perish at the hands of cruel and unprincipled men.   In the day when those "who sleep in the dust of the earth shall awake," all these apparent anomalies shall be rectified.   Then the right shall come uppermost.   Then justice shall be done.   Then shall the crown be given to those who on earth were nailed to the cross of ignominy, or trampled under the heel of oppression; while the wicked, who on earth seemed so exalted, shall have as his portion "shame and everlasting contempt."

Thus, viewed in connection with the final judgment, the doctrine of the resurrection of the dead is not only a support to those who are suffering wrongfully, but also a warning to all who are dealing unrighteously with God and his people. The present life is connected most intimately and inseparably with that which is to come. *Now* is for every one of us the germ of *hereafter;* and "whatsoever a man soweth" on earth, "that shall he also reap" in the future state. The awards to be made on the day of resurrection are not things of caprice. They are the outcome and development of the characters which we have formed and the conduct which we have practised in the life of probation which has been granted us on earth. Our future destiny will be, in the case of each of us, as much the natural outgrowth of our present character as the ripened stalk is of the corn of wheat which we cast into the soil. We often speak of the day of judgment, indeed, as the day for which all other days were made; but it would be more correct to call it that which all other days are making. It will make nothing new. It will only reveal and make indelible the results of the old. We are making it now. We are even at this present time laying up for ourselves eternal glory or everlasting contempt.

"The tissue of the life to be, we weave with colors all our own,
And in the field of destiny we reap as we have sown ;
Still shall the soul around it call the shadows which it gathered here,
And, painted on the eternal wall, the past shall reappear."

Oh, my brethren, with what importance does this consideration invest the present life! Every thought we think, every action we perform, every word we speak, every opportunity of usefulness improved or neglected, is a seed sown by us, the fruit of which shall meet us either in richest blessing or in untold misery, in the eternity into which we go. And yet, how little we think of all this, and how seldom we act under the influence which these truths are fitted to produce and foster within us!

In the stirring days of English martyrology, we read of one eminent victim, that when he had been brought from his

dungeon to a magnificent chamber hung all around with richest tapestry, and was being gradually drawn into a conversation concerning himself and his fellow-confessors, he heard
the sound of the nib of a pen moving upon paper behind the
arras, as if one were writing there in concealment, and in a
moment he became silent, for well he knew that a thought-
less word might bring down upon himself or upon his companions the severest woes. But, brethren, though we hear
it not, a record of all we think and say and do is being
taken; yea, we ourselves are writing it on the tablets of our
memories and hearts—and the effects shall be eternal. What
need, then, of prudence and prayerfulness, that so these consequences may bring to us eternal life, and not shame and
everlasting contempt. It is told of Zeuxis, the famous paint-
er, that he was remarkable for the pains which he bestowed
upon his works, and that on one occasion, when he was accused of being long in drawing his lines, and slow in the
use of his pencil, he replied, "I am long in doing what I
take in hand, because I want to do it with care; for what I
paint, I paint for eternity." Beloved, shall this be so in the
case of one seeking permanent earthly fame? and shall not
we be infinitely more careful in our words and ways, knowing that we are making ourselves for eternity? Let us see
to it that we so finish our life-work here that when we are
confronted with it on the resurrection morn, we may not be
filled with everlasting shame; and to this end, let us live for
Christ; for where he is, there is life and glory.

But we have here, secondly, the reward of the working
saint. "They that be wise shall shine as the brightness of
the firmament; and they that turn many to righteousness,
as the stars for ever and ever." I do not know whether there
be any implied comparison here between the wise and those
who turn many to righteousness, or whether the design of
the angel is to represent that the glory of the one tran-

scends that of the other.   Possibly the two clauses may form
one parallelism, after the manner of the Hebrew poets.   We
remember, at least, that Solomon hath said, " He that win-
neth souls is wise ;" and perhaps the celestial speaker here
refers to the same class of persons in both the expressions
which he has employed.   But however that question may
be decided, I take out of the verse what is undeniably in it,
when I say that they who turn many to righteousness will
be honored with bright and particular glory in the heavenly
state.   " They shine as the stars for ever and ever."   Here
is the grand aim toward which Christian ambition should be
directed.   If there be any rivalry or competition among us,
it ought to be, as to which of us shall convert the greatest
number of sinners "from the error of their ways," and shine
the most lustrously in the firmament of the future.   Earthly
ambition seeks to gain something for itself, and too often
it rises to its greatest elevation by trampling others down ;
but the glory of the Christian is to be attained by saving
and serving men.   Here is the law: "He that will be greatest among you, let him be your servant ; even as the Son of
man came, not to be ministered unto, but to minister, and
to give his life a ransom for many."   This is the great fun-
damental distinction between the world-kingdoms of which
in this book so much has been said, and the kingdom of
Christ, by which, at length, they are all to be superseded.

Among the nations of the earth decorations and honors
are given to those who have done the greatest work of destruction.   Nebuchadnezzar, Cyrus, Alexander, Cæsar, all
rose to their proud pre-eminence through the crushing force
of that physical power which they brought to bear upon
their rivals.   They waded through blood to their thrones ;
and the steps up which they mounted to their elevation
consisted of the bodies of their prostrate foes.   But in the
kingdom of Christ it is far otherwise.   The places of pre-

eminence under him are assigned to those who have been
likest him in the holiness of their characters, in the self-
sacrifice of their lives, and in the hallowing and ennobling
influence which they have shed around them. They who
have done the most in the diffusion of righteousness, by
their own character and efforts ; they who have fought, not
with carnal weapons, but with spiritual, against cruelty and
wrong, and injustice, and iniquity of every form ; they who,
by the diffusion of the light of the Gospel, and through the
might of the Holy Ghost, have been instrumental in trans-
forming the greatest number of their fellows from the vota-
ries of wickedness into the followers of righteousness : these
are they who shall sit nearest the throne of Jesus when he
cometh in his kingdom.

Oh, what a firmament is that wherein these orbs are
placed, and by how many " bright particular stars " is it already gemmed !   There are Paul and Peter, and John and
Timothy, and Polycarp and Chrysostom, and Augustine and
Athanasius, and Luther and Latimer, and Calvin and Knox,
and Wesley and Whitefield, and McCheyne and Burns, and
Edwards and Payson, and Nettleton and Harlan Page.
There, too, are multitudes who, unassuming and almost un-
known on earth, kept working on, their grandeur and nobleness revealed to themselves only when they went into the
Saviour's presence.   My brethren, is there nothing here to
attract you ?   What are all the titles and rewards of earth,
compared with this undying honor from the hand of Christ ?
Be it yours to strive for that.   Let no difficulty appal you ;
let no danger keep you back ; let righteousness be the girdle of your own loins, and live to make others righteous
through the diffusion of the Gospel of regeneration and
holiness.   " Get all the good you can, do all the good you
can, to all that you can, and as long as you can ;" and then,
when you go hence, you will be greeted with the welcome,

"Well done, good and faithful servant: enter thou into the joy of thy Lord."

Finally, we have here the rest of the waiting saint: "Go thou thy way till the end be: for thou shalt rest, and stand in thy lot at the end of the days." How prone we are to trouble ourselves about the future! Yea, even after we have received the assurances which God has given us in his word, we are apt, like Daniel, to cry, "What shall be the end of these things?" We may be worried about personal affairs; we may be distressed about the after-lot of our children; or, with a degree of public spirit, we may be anxious about what shall emerge either in the State or in the Church. Now, to each of those who are in this uncomfortable condition of heart, provided they be the people of God, we are warranted to say, "Go thou thy way till the end be: for thou shalt rest, and stand in thy lot at the end of the days." Do not disquiet yourself about the future. Leave that in God's hands. You shall rest in him during the remainder of your life on earth; and when that shall end, you shall rest with him. Nay, more; at the consummation of all things you shall stand in your lot, having God himself as your inheritance. Nothing can really harm us if we are united to God, through faith in Jesus Christ. What says Paul?—and he had passed through trials enough before he wrote the words, so that we may regard him as speaking with the authority of experience—"I am persuaded that neither death, nor life, nor angels, nor principalities, nor powers, nor things present, nor things to come, nor height, nor depth, nor any other creature, shall be able to separate us from the love of God which is in Christ Jesus our Lord." Let us wait patiently, therefore, upon him. Though things around us may seem full of threatening, God is over all; though things within us may be tremulous and desponding, God is in us, and he will be our strength; though things before us may look dark and lowering, God will go forward with us, and make all safe for us. Why, then, should we be afraid? Go thy way, forlorn and weary one. Go thy way, and rest in God. Let him think and plan for thee ; and then when the end of the days shall come, thou shalt be found in the lot of heaven's inheritance. Trust in God, for that is rest on earth. Wait on God, and he will give thee the higher rest of the better land.

XIII.

THE CHARACTER OF DANIEL.

Daniel x., 11.

"O Daniel, a man greatly beloved."

OUR later studies in this book have been so entirely devoted to the wonderful series of predictions with which it concludes, that we have, to some extent, lost sight of the man to whom these prophecies were communicated at the first, and by whom they were transmitted to others. It is fitting, therefore, that in closing our series of discourses on this portion of the Word of God, and while yet the recorded incidents of Daniel's life are fresh in our recollection, we should endeavor to give you some analysis of his character as that has revealed itself to us during our examination of his work.

That work was as noble as it was peculiar. Called, at the beginning of the Babylonian Captivity, to witness for Jehovah, he was honored to maintain a blameless record throughout the entire seventy years of the exile, and to take a principal part in the events which led to the famous edict of Cyrus, by which permission was given to the Jews to return to their own land. He lived thus through a critical era in the history of his nation. He was tried by adversity, and by the more searching test of sudden prosperity; yet he was always true to the convictions of his conscience, and faithful to the commandments of his God. Though in the world of Babylon, he was not of it; his heart was ever holding fellowship with Jehovah; and the temptations to honor and emolument were as impotent to move him as were the flames of the furnace or the lions of the den.

One cannot read the earlier chapters of this book without having recalled to memory another exile in another land, who through the same "patient continuance in well-doing," under suffering and temptation, rose to the second position in the State, and lived to be the savior of his people in a time of strait. Of Daniel, as of Joseph, it was true that "the Lord gave him favor in the sight" of those who were above him, and raised him to honor through the interpretation of a monarch's dreams; and of both alike it might be said that they wore

> "The white flower of a blameless life,
> In that fierce light which beats upon a throne,
> And blackens every blot."

But when we come upon such an expression as that which I have chosen as my text, we are made to think of "that disciple whom Jesus loved," and who "leaned upon his breast" at the Last Supper, rather than of any Old Testament worthy. And indeed there are many points of resemblance between these two seers. Both were peculiarly dear to the heart of God; and because "the secret of the Lord is with them that fear him," to both were revealed more clearly than to others "the things which are written" in the book of the divine purposes. In their relation to their fellow-servants they occupied a position of remarkable similarity. If, among the evangelists, Matthew may be said to have had the face of the ox, and Mark that of the lion, and Luke that of the man, to John must be ascribed that of the eagle, whose eye looks undazzled at the brightness of the sun, and sees afar the minutest objects with distinctness. But the same is true of Daniel, as connected with Isaiah, Jeremiah, and Ezekiel. The son of Amos is the ox, with his patient, plodding endurance; Jeremiah is the man, with the tear of sorrow in his eye, or the tone of denunciation in his speech; Ezekiel is the lion, with his mien of majesty and voice of thunder; but Daniel is the eagle, "whose nest is on high," and "whose eyes behold afar off."

Yet, reminding us though he does of John, the beloved disciple and apocalyptic seer, Daniel has an official greatness distinct even from that of the prophet of Patmos. His predictions took their character from his position in life. He was educated in earthly kingdoms, that he might tell of the higher greatness of the kingdom of Christ. We owe to him, more than to any others of his brethren in the Old Testament, our ideas of the royalty of Jesus. His "prophetic watch-tower," as Auberlen has finely said, "was erected beside the throne of Babylon; and standing there in, and yet above, the first world-monarchy, he looked out into the farthest future, and discerned with prophetic eye, which God had opened, the changing shapes and events of coming kingdoms,"* and the growing glory and ultimate triumph of the kingdom of Christ. Thus his distinctive prophetic mission grew out of, or was grafted upon, his position in public life; but that, again, was the result of his personal character; and so we are led most naturally to the consideration of his individual peculiarities.

Among these I mention, first, *his early piety*. We know little of his parents. It comes out incidentally that he was of the seed-royal; but he was taken away from his home, and from his country, while yet he was a boy. As we saw in our first lecture, he could not have been more than fourteen years of age when, with his three companions, he was sent to be educated at the college of the Chaldeans. Yet even then he had learned to love Jehovah, and to make the divine law the rule of his life. Now, I am particular in giv-

---

* "Daniel and the Revelation," by Carl August Auberlen, etc., p. 21.

ing prominence to this fact; for it has come to be believed by the young people of our day that early piety is a simpering, sentimental thing, betokening the existence in its subject both of physical and mental weakness. Much of this common and pernicious heresy must, I fear, be traced to the influence of our popular Sunday-school literature; for in the books which are put into the hands of our children it is too often the case that when we read of a winning and obedient child, who is distinguished for purity and devotion to God, we find that his life came to a premature end. Thus the idea is fostered that when one becomes, in the years of his boyhood, an earnest Christian, he is "too good for this world," and is removed as soon as may be to a better. Now, such books are pre-eminently unhealthy, because they are untrue; and the mischief is that, in the great majority of instances, they repel their readers from religion altogether. Our young people do not want to become Christians if their history is to be of that sort. They are conscious of the possession of overflowing vitality, and they have, besides, the natural, and indeed laudable, ambition to do something in the world. They shrink from a life of physical weakness, and from an early death; and therefore they should be told not simply of the piety of those who have died in childhood, but also, and even more fully, of that of those who lived, it may be, to a good old age, and who were honored to do good and noble service for God and for their generation. Now, this is to them a very great attraction in the history of Daniel. He gave himself to the Lord while he was a boy, yet he lived to be well-nigh ninety years old.

And his piety did not interfere with his pre-eminence. He was, shall I say? the valedictorian of his year. He held all through the very highest place in his class, and was not the less distinguished as a student because he was so prominent in the matter of religion. Nay, his elevation, as we see in the various incidents of his career, was closely connected with his piety. No doubt he had to suffer for his religion ; for it was true then, as it is now, that all who will live godly in the world must suffer persecution of some sort; but still he proved it to be true that "godliness is profitable unto all things, having promise of the life that now is, and of that which is to come." Nor was there any element of feebleness about him. He was healthy alike in body and in mind ; and in his conduct in the matter of the meat and the wine that came from the royal table, there were those characteristics of pluck and manliness which have always been so attractive and so stimulating to young men. He had the courage not only to have convictions, but also to act upon them ; and that courage, so far from standing in the way of his promotion, was one of the things which contributed to it.

I desire, therefore, to call the attention of my youthful hearers to these points. You will make a terrible mistake if you suppose that piety unfits you for life, or imagine that its existence in youth is an abnormal thing that indicates the presence of disease. Believe me, there is nothing so healthy, or so wholesome, as to give yourselves early to the Lord. It will lay in you the foundation of a vigorous and energetic character. It will bring the highest of all motives to bear alike upon education, recreation, and business, and enable you to make the very best of yourselves for God and for your fellow-men. It will secure for you all that is best worth having in the world, while, along with that, you will have the enjoyment of God's favor, and the prospect of heaven's happiness. For the case of Daniel is not exceptional. You have the same things illustrated in the lives of Joseph and Moses and Samuel, and in some degree, also, in that of Timothy ; while, if you care to look around you and inquire into the histories of many of those among ourselves who are most loved and trusted by their fellow-citizens, you will discover that they also have "feared God from their youth."

Nor can I refrain from adding that, in all such individuals, there is a full, rounded completeness of character, a well-balanced equilibrium of disposition, which you look for in vain in those who have been converted in later life.   In these last, indeed, you will often find some marked excellences.   They will be very earnest and enthusiastic; they may be very liberal, and self-sacrificing; but there is usually in them also some prominent angularity, which mars the rotundity of their nature, and prevents them from doing or enjoying as much as those who, like Daniel, have been from their boyhood devoted to the Lord.

From every point of view, therefore, the history of Daniel is encouraging to the young.   It bids them consecrate themselves to the Saviour ere yet "the cares of the world," or "the deceitfulness of riches," or the engagements of business have stolen away their hearts.   It shows them that the world's prizes may be gained by one who means to lay them in the lap of Christ.   It proves to them that manliness is by no means incompatible with godliness, and that the loftiest intellectual culture may be reached while yet the student is sitting lowly at the feet of Jesus; while, on the other side, it is full of loftiest inspiration to parents and teachers. There are those who sneer at piety in boyhood, as if it would soon die out, and leave the soul more hardened than it would have been if no such emotions had ever entered it. But who will sneer at Daniel?   Were not his parents more than rewarded for their exertions in his early religious training by the noble stand he made, and the lofty elevation he reached?   And when, though he could then have been no more than forty years of age, Ezekiel the prophet singled him out for special commendation, placing him beside Noah

and Job, was there not given the strongest possible endorsement to the efforts and the prayers of those who are seeking the early conversion of their children? "The man
greatly beloved" began himself to love God in his boyhood.

I mention, secondly, among Daniel's characteristics, *his
devoutness in the closet.* This comes out first in connection with the recovery and interpretation of Nebuchadnezzar's forgotten dream; for then not only did he engage
his three friends to pray on his behalf, but he also himself
poured out his heart in thanksgiving to Jehovah. But it
was the habit of his life to wait at stated times on God; for
when his enemies prevailed on Darius to issue that decree
which forbade any one to pray save unto the king, we are
told that "he kneeled upon his knees three times a day,
and prayed, and gave thanks before his God, as aforetime."
His custom was to observe these appointed seasons of devotion; and from the record which we have in the ninth
chapter of his study of the prophecies of Jeremiah, we are
warranted in concluding that when he was in his closet, he
gave himself to meditation on the Sacred Scriptures, as well
as to earnest supplication. This helps to explain much of
his conduct. We cease to wonder at his boldness before
Nebuchadnezzar, Belshazzar, and Darius, when we learn
that he maintained such constant communion with his God.
The roots of his character were "mellowed and fattened"
by the dews of heavenly influence which fell upon them
in the closet. He drew his strength from the heaven with
which he was in such continuous communication. He was
"Daniel," the judge of God; because he was first "Israel," a
prince of God, who prevailed with him in prayer. His public life was holy and incorruptible, because his hidden life
was prayerful and devout. He carried his business habits
with him into the closet; and so he was enabled to carry
his devout spirit with him into business. His life was not

divided into two portions, separated from each other like the water-tight compartments in a ship; but it was one and the same everywhere. In the closet, he was transacting business with God; in the presidential bureau, he was transacting business for God; and his sincerity in the former enabled him to maintain faithfulness in the latter.

Now, here we may all learn much from him. Amidst the rush and hurry of our modern life, the closet is apt to be neglected.

> "The world is too much with us:
> Getting and spending, we lay waste our powers."

And the recreative influence of devotional retirement is neither sought nor valued as it ought to be. But we cannot go on thus without deterioration. Sooner or later, the freshness will wear off from our spirits; the keen edge of our consciences will be blunted; and the general level of our conduct will be lowered. We need to have our hearts constantly purified by communion with God; otherwise the contamination of the world will cleave to them, and they will "become subdued to that they work in, like the dyer's hand." Hence, to counteract the influence of the age, we ought to give now more than ever prominence to the exercises of the closet. Instead of overlaying the Bible with other books, we ought to go more frequently to its refreshing pages; and while we do not in the least disparage the habit of ejaculatory prayer, we ought to give more time and attention to supplications in the closet. They give a tonic to the piety of the heart, and a stimulus to the life of the day, which we cannot miss without detriment; and when men tell us, as they sometimes do, that the highest style of living is when we are always in a prayerful spirit, even although we have no set times for devotion, we are tempted to reply that it is impossible to maintain a devotional spirit without having an appointed time for its cultivation.

He whose apostle said, " Pray without ceasing," said himself, " When thou prayest, enter into thy closet, and shut thy door ;" and the hour of private devotion is as essential to the preservation of the spirituality of the day as the holy rest of the Sabbath is to the maintenance of the piety of the week. Periodicity is one of the laws of our being. The tear and wear of the day needs to be repaired by the sleep of the night ; and the exhaustion consequent upon labor must be removed by the taking of food at regular and stated intervals.   So, also, the spiritual waste of the day must be repaired by the exercises of the closet ; and every one who has tried this specific can say for himself, with David, " He restoreth my soul ; he leadeth me in the paths of righteousness for his name's sake."

It is no answer to all this to allege that the habits of society, and the demands of business upon us, are such that we cannot find opportunity for retirement. That is only a confession that the necessity for it is most urgent ; for we need it the most just then when it is hardest to take it. Hence, in these days, we ought to value the closet even more than our fathers did. They had abundance of leisure. No clicking telegraph followed them everywhere with its messages ; no whistling steam-engine hurried all their movements ; the postman was not forever ringing at their doors ; and the clamorous deputation was not continually in their parlors seeking a contribution or an address. Yet they delighted in meditation and prayer, and felt themselves strengthened by their influence. Oh, how much more we need them than they did ! But how little we plan for them, and how slightly we relish them ! Brethren, this is all wrong.   I repeat the warning : We cannot go on at this rate without spiritual deterioration ! Do not tell me that this is a *practical* age. It is so only because a thoughtful and devotional age preceded it ; and if we eliminate the de-

votion and the meditation out of it, we shall soon destroy
its practicalness.   The inspiration which gives us wisdom
to discern, and ability to do, and happiness to enjoy our
work, comes from the closet, and if we more fully realized
that fact, we should more seldom be inclined to say, " I
have no time for private. prayer."   As well might the manu-
facturer say that he has no time to kindle the fire which is
to raise the steam that is to drive his machinery!   No time
for the closet!   Say, rather, " I have no time to eat," or, " I
have no time to sleep."   Yea, let the hours consecrated to
secret fellowship with God be the very last which you will
allow either fashion or business to crowd in upon or in-
fringe.

I mention as another distinctive feature of Daniel his *decision of character*.   When the unclean articles of diet were
set before him, he did not hesitate as to the course which
he would follow.   Come what would, he was determined
that he should not touch them.   True, he very prudently
made application to the prince of the eunuchs in the matter.
Yet he had already purposed in his heart that he would not
defile himself ; and this conduct of his, in his youth, enables
us to understand the valor of his later life, when he braved
the fury of the lions rather than give up the privilege of
prayer.   Of what good would longer earthly existence have
been, when that which gave it its charm and inspiration was
no longer to be enjoyed by him ?   So this habit of decision
grew up in him, and was fed in him, by the communion of
the closet, whereof we have already spoken.   He learned
there to look at things as in the sight of God ; and he carried that test with him through life.   He acted " as seeing
him who is invisible."   God was more to him than all else ;
and that made it easy for him to decide questions which to
others would have been difficult, and to brave dangers which
to others would have been appalling.   This sense of the

divine presence, and assurance of the divine favor, lifted him above the influences of the world, and kept him ever on the side of the right and the true. It made no matter what men threatened—God was on his side; and so he was not terrified. It made no matter what men promised—God was already his; and so it was impossible to bribe him. The man who had heard these words from the lips of Gabriel, "O man greatly beloved," could not be allured by any title of worldly dignity or any token of mortal favor. He lived above all these things; so he could speak with calm faithfulness to Nebuchadnezzar and Belshazzar, and look with composure on the lions of Darius. He saw not the grandeur of the former by reason of the greater glory of Jehovah; and he feared not the fury of the latter by reason of his confidence in the omnipotence of God.

It is easier to describe such a life, and to understand how it could be lived, than it is to reproduce it. And yet the God of Daniel liveth; there is no change in him. Only we lack the faith of Daniel, and from that lack all our difficulties spring. Could we but "see him who is invisible," we might rival him whose faith "stopped the mouths of lions." The child is brave when he knows his father is by his side; and we should feel it easy to do right, and to brave danger, if we could only believe that God is with us of a truth. The prophet's servant understood his master's composure in a moment when his eyes were opened to see, what his master's faith had seen all the while, namely, "chariots of fire and horses of fire round about him." And if we only believe in the presence with us of our reconciled God and Father in Jesus Christ, no bribe could allure us to sin, and no threat could terrify us to commit iniquity. "This is the victory that overcometh the world, even our faith."

We complicate matters so long as we take into account only the opinions of men, or the probable social results of our actions. But when we see God, we become indifferent to all these things, and decide only according to his will. Is it not so, my friends? Do not all our perplexities arise from earthly considerations? Have we ever any hesitation as to how we ought to act when we look at the question entirely as between us and God? And if that be so, ought we not to acquire the habit of acting always as seeing "him who is invisible." Before him all subterfuges flee, and all disguises disappear. We cannot juggle with our consciences while we feel that he is near. We cannot parley with the tempter while he is at our side; and if he will say to us as he did to Daniel, "O man greatly beloved," there is no longer any charm in the applause of men that shall win us from his allegiance. Thus decision of character is intimately connected with—nay, directly springs from—faith in the presence, the protection, and the favor of God.

Young men, will you lay that to heart? Your strength to resist temptation depends on the positiveness of your conviction that there is a God, and that he is your God through Jesus Christ. Oh, what power would fill your souls, not only for withstanding evil, but also for cultivating holiness, if but you would realize what Hagar meant when she said, "Thou, God, seest me!" He whom she thus addressed was no dogging detective, come to upbraid her with her sin, and to apprehend her for punishment, but a loving father who gave to her the soothing solace of his sympathy, and the gracious promise of his love and care; and if we could only rise to the assurance that he is our own God, through Jesus Christ, we would welcome his presence as a source of strength and an element of power. It is easy to decide and to be firm when we know and believe that God is near.

Another distinctive feature of Daniel was *his diligence in business*. As a student his industry was so great that he easily overtopped his fellows, and in the management of imperial affairs he developed a faculty for organization, and evinced an energy and perseverance that were beyond all praise. After a time of devotion, we read that "he arose and did the king's business;" and the principles on which he conducted the department that was entrusted to his care may be inferred from the fact that, when his enemies sought an occasion against him, they could find nothing wrong in his office, and had to endeavor to entrap him in the matter of his God. He had his ups and downs, like others, but in the main he was what even the world would call a successful man, and his prosperity was not the result of any accident, but was the consequence of the perseverance and integrity by which he was distinguished.

Nor is it at all unimportant, in these days, that prominence should be given to these facts. For the common idea among many is that religion and business are incompatible. If one have the reputation of being a godly man, he is at once written down as unfitted for the highest kind of commercial success. On the other hand, if one have risen to eminence in mercantile life, it is supposed that he cannot be a very devout man; and if he make the profession of being so, he is summarily characterized as a hypocrite. Now, these ideas are as injurious to business as they are to religion, and I am glad to have so excellent an opportunity of denouncing them as false. Daniel was no hypocrite, and yet he rose, deservedly, to the highest position which Babylon had to give. And, when we look at the matter candidly, we must admit that religion, so far from being inimical to his business success, was a powerful and important factor in its production.

Why should the cultivation of the heart be inconsistent with eminence in commerce any more than the gratification of a taste for literature? Yet how many men, honored on our exchanges or in our assemblies, are devoted also to the prosecution of literary pursuits! The noblest statesman that England has seen for more than a generation has been able, without at all detracting from his eminence, either as a financial reformer or as a prime minister, to find time for the cultivation of Homeric studies, and for the unearthing of the designs of Vaticanism. And, in our own city, the patriarch of letters who is making the writings of Homer into American classics is known also as one of the most successful of newspaper editors. If, therefore, men may cultivate the head without entailing upon themselves a business failure, why may they not also cultivate the heart?

But, more than this, the very duties of business furnish an opportunity for the fostering of religion. For what is religion? Is it not, above all other things, THE SCIENCE OF CHARACTER? Is it not the process of self-formation, according to the purest model, and from the loftiest motives? And if that be so, does not public life give the noblest opportunities for its practice? Whatever we do, and wherever we are, we are making or manifesting character, and we must do so either in the right way or in the wrong. Religion is the doing of this in the right way; and if that be incompatible with prosperity in business, then all I have to say is, so much the worse for business. But it is not incompatible with business success. It may not give a rapid fortune, indeed, but that is not a misfortune; for these rapid fortunes often end in the prison, or in exile. But it has often given, and it will give again, a solid, substantial, and enduring prosperity, which no persecution can destroy, and no panic can sweep away.

Nor is this all. Consider what religion does for a man. It brings him under the influence of the most powerful motives. As we have seen already, it opens his eyes to the sight of the invisible God; and so it sends him to work for him. But is there anything in that to paralyze industry, or to overlay diligence? Nay, verily, he who is doing business for God will always be in earnest. . His diligence in business will be a part of his religion, and he will enjoy the fulfilment of the proverb, that "the hand of the diligent maketh rich." True, his religion will keep him from all double-dealing and dishonesty, and so he may not rise so rapidly as the wicked sometimes do; but then, neither will he fall so swiftly and ignominiously as they. He will go by the king's highway, not through any short cuts; and if he do not reach the goal so soon as others seem to do, he is saved from being mired in the morass, in which they shall surely sink.

Believe not, therefore, my young friends, that your allegiance to God will ultimately interfere with your commercial success. Even if it did, it would still be your duty to be true to him. But it does not. God's providence is moral, and if you make a fair induction of facts, you will find that, other things being equal, the religious man is in the end the most prosperous as well as the most happy of merchants. I know this is a low view to take of it. But I know, also, that the assertions which I have referred to are made by those who would seduce you from the paths of integrity; and therefore I have taken the trouble to refute their reasonings. Do not allow yourselves to be led away by their plausibilities; probe them to the bottom; examine them with the keenest scrutiny, and you will remain true to Christ, who has said not only, "Blessed are the pure in heart, for they shall see God;" but also, "Blessed are the meek, for they shall inherit the earth."

But here we must conclude. We have had great enjoyment in tracing the history and studying the prophecies of this man of God. We have learned to know his principles, and he has taught us to know our Christ as "the King of kings and Lord of lords." Let us pray for his faith, and let us cultivate his devotional spirit. Then we shall be able to manifest his firmness in the face of temptation, and to practise his diligence in the details of common life. Let us carry his business energy into our religious duties, and his devout spirit into our business transactions. Let us live as he did, as seeing him who is invisible, saying, with the noble poet,

"All is, if we have grace to use it, so
As ever in the great Task-master's eye,"

and then we, too, "shall stand in our lot at the end of the days."

INDEX.

THE END.